THE GREATEST MYSTERIES IN HISTORY

101 of the Most Mind-Boggling Mysteries Ever!

SUSAN BURKE

ISBN: 978-1-962496-12-4

For questions, please reach out to <u>Support@OakHarborPress.com</u>

Please consider leaving a review!

Just visit: OakHarborPress.com/Reviews

FREE BONUS

SCAN TO GET OUR NEXT BOOK FOR FREE!

TABLE OF CONTENTS

INTRODUCTION 1

CHAPTER ONE: COSMIC CONUNDRUMS 3

[1] THE BLACK KNIGHT SATELLITE: ORIGINS AND TRACKING 4

[2] UFO SIGHTINGS THROUGHOUT HISTORY: ROSWELL TO RENDLESAM FOREST 5

[3] DARK MATTER AND DARK ENERGY: THE UNIVERSE'S UNSEEN FORCES 6

[4] THE TUNGUSKA EVENT: A MYSTERIOUS EXPLOSION IN SIBERIA 7

[5] THE PIONEER ANOMALY: UNEXPLAINED DEVIATIONS IN SPACECRAFT TRAJECTORIES 8

[6] TABBY'S STAR: A STAR'S MYSTERIOUS DIMMING PATTERN 9

[7] THE SEARCH FOR PLANET NINE: BEYOND NEPTUNE'S ORBIT 10

[8] FAST RADIO BURSTS: UNEXPLAINED COSMIC SIGNALS 11

[9] THEORIES ON MULTIVERSES: ARE THERE PARALLEL UNIVERSES? 12

CHAPTER TWO: ANCIENT ANOMALIES 13

[10] ADVANCED ANCIENT TECHNOLOGIES: THE BAGHDAD BATTERY AND ANTIKYTHERA MECHANISM 14

[11] THE SACSAYHUAMÁN WALLS: PRECISELY CARVED STONES 15

[12] THE MOAI OF EASTER ISLAND: TRANSPORT THEORIES 16

[13] THE ORIGINS OF THE SPHINX: WATER EROSION CONTROVERSY 17

[14] GÖBEKLI TEPE: WORLD'S OLDEST TEMPLE OR ASTRONOMICAL OBSERVATORY? 18

[15] THE DROPA STONES: ANCIENT ALIEN ARTIFACTS? 19

[16] THE PIRI REIS MAP: AN ANCIENT MYSTERY 20

[17] THE RONGORONGO SCRIPT OF EASTER ISLAND: UNDECIPHERED SYMBOLS 21

[18] THE MYTHS OF EL DORADO: QUEST FOR THE CITY OF GOLD 22

CHAPTER THREE: MYSTERIOUS CREATURES 24

[19] EL CHUPACABRA: ORIGINS AND DESCRIPTIONS 25

[20] MERMAIDS AND MERMEN: SIGHTINGS AND MYTHS 26

[21] THE JERSEY DEVIL: HIDDEN IN THE PINE BARRENS 27

[22] MOKELE-MBEMBE: AFRICA'S MYTHICAL DINOSAUR? 28

[23] THUNDERBIRDS: GIANT BIRDS OF NATIVE AMERICAN LORE 29

[24] YOWIE AND YETI: BIGFOOT'S INTERNATIONAL COUSINS 30

[25] GIGANTIC SEA SERPENTS: REPORTS AND MYTHS 31

[26] MOTHMAN: THE MYSTERY 32

[27] THE LOVELAND FROG: HIDDEN IN OHIO....................33

[28] LAKE MONSTERS AROUND THE WORLD: CHAMP, OGOPOGO, AND MORE..34

CHAPTER FOUR: DISAPPEARING ACTS....................................37

[29] THE BERMUDA TRIANGLE: HISTORICAL DISAPPEARANCES AND THEORIES....................................38

[30] FLIGHT MH370: THE SEQUENCE OF EVENTS AND INVESTIGATION 39

[31] THE ROANOKE COLONY: THEORIES AND CLUES LEFT BEHIND...40

[32] THE SODDER CHILDREN DISAPPEARANCE: A FAMILY'S RELENTLESS SEARCH...41

[33] THE FLANNAN ISLES LIGHTHOUSE KEEPERS: ABANDONED IN A STORM?...42

[34] THE ANGIKUNI LAKE DISAPPEARANCE: AN ENTIRE VILLAGE VANISHES 43

[35] FREDERICK VALENTICH: A PILOT'S UNEXPLAINED MID-FLIGHT DISAPPEARANCE..44

[36] THE MISSING NINTH LEGION OF ROME: A LEGION LOST TO HISTORY 45

[37] THE COPPER SCROLL: A LOST TREASURE...................46

[38] THE VANISHING OF PERCY FAWCETT: AN EXPLORER'S QUEST FOR THE CITY OF Z..............................47

CHAPTER FIVE: CRYPTIC CODES AND LANGUAGES...........49

[39] THE VOYNICH MANUSCRIPT: ORIGINS AND PURPOSE 50

[40] THE ZODIAC KILLER'S CYPHERS: PARTIALLY SOLVED MESSAGES.. 51

[41] *KRYPTOS*: THE UNSOLVED SCULPTURE AT CIA HEADQUARTERS... 52

[42] THE PHAISTOS DISK: A MINOAN MYSTERY 53

[43] LINEAR A: THE UNDECIPHERED MINOAN SCRIPT ... 54

[44] THE TAMÁM SHUD CASE: A MAN, A CODE, AND AN UNSOLVED DEATH... 55

[45] THE D' AGAPEYEFF CIPHER: AN UNSOLVED CRYPTOGRAM.. 56

[46] THE RICKY MCCORMICK NOTES: ENCRYPTED MESSAGES OR GIBBERISH?...................................... 57

[47] THE BEALE CIPHERS: TREASURE OR TALL TALE? 58

[48] THE DORABELLA CIPHER: ELGAR'S MYSTERIOUS NOTE 59

CHAPTER SIX: HAUNTING HISTORIES 61

[49] THE GHOSTS OF THE TOWER OF LONDON: ANNE BOLEYN AND MORE... 62

[50] THE *MARY CELESTE*: THEORIES ON THE DISAPPEARING CREW 63

[51] THE AMITYVILLE HAUNTING: SORTING FACTS FROM FICTION 64

[52] THE BELL WITCH: A POLTERGEIST IN TENNESSEE ... 65

[53] THE CHASE FAMILY CRYPT: COFFINS THAT WOULDN'T STAY PUT... 66

[54] THE BROWN LADY OF RAYNHAM HALL: THE FAMOUS GHOST PHOTOGRAPH 67

[55] BORLEY RECTORY: THE MOST HAUNTED HOUSE IN ENGLAND 68

[56] THE MYRTLES PLANTATION: A HAUNTED HISTORY 69

[57] THE TALE OF LA LLORONA: A WEEPING SPIRIT 70

[58] THE HAUNTINGS OF THE STANLEY HOTEL: INSPIRATION FOR *THE SHINING* 71

CHAPTER SEVEN: HISTORICAL ENIGMAS 73

[59] STONEHENGE: CONSTRUCTION AND ALIGNMENT THEORIES 74

[60] THE SHROUD OF TURIN: SCIENTIFIC INVESTIGATIONS AND DEBATES 75

[61] THE TERRACOTTA ARMY: CREATION AND UNKNOWN CHAMBERS 76

[62] PRINCES IN THE TOWER: DISAPPEARANCES AND DEATHS 77

[63] THE DANCING PLAGUE OF 1518: ORIGINS AND THEORIES 78

[64] THE OSEBERG SHIP BURIAL: A VIKING ENIGMA 79

[65] THE VINLAND MAP: AUTHENTIC OR FORGERY? 80

[66] THE SEA PEOPLES: THE UNKNOWN INVADERS OF ANCIENT CIVILIZATIONS 81

[67] CLEOPATRA'S LOST TOMB: AN ANCIENT MYSTERY 82

[68] THE ARK OF THE COVENANT: UNCERTAIN FATE 83

CHAPTER EIGHT: POLITICAL PUZZLES 85

[69] THE JFK ASSASSINATION: THE GRASSY KNOLL AND THE MAGIC BULLET THEORY 86

[70] THE FATE OF THE AMBER ROOM: THEORIES OF ITS CURRENT LOCATION 87

[71] JIMMY HOFFA'S LAST DAYS: LEADS, SPECULATIONS, AND FALSE CLAIMS 88

[72] NAPOLEON BONAPARTE: THE NOTORIOUS LEADER'S CAUSE OF DEATH 89

[73] MARTIN BORMANN'S DISAPPEARANCE: ESCAPE, SIGHTINGS, AND DNA 90

[74] GRAND DUCHESS ANASTASIA: DID SHE ESCAPE THE BOLSHEVIKS? 92

[75] LORD LUCAN: CIRCUMSTANCES AND DISAPPEARANCE 93

[76] DAG HAMMARKJÖLD: MYSTERIOUS DEATH OF A UN SECRETARY-GENERAL 94

CHAPTER NINE: UNIDENTIFIED PHENOMENA 97

[77] CROP CIRCLES: HUMAN OR UNKNOWN ORIGINS.... 98

[78] THE TAOS HUM: INVESTIGATIVE REPORTS AND THEORIES.. 99

[79] THE HESSDALEN LIGHTS: NORWAY'S UNEXPLAINED LUMINOUS PHENOMENON.................................... 100

[80] SKYQUAKES: POSSIBLE EXPLANATIONS 101

[81] THE BLUE PEOPLE OF KENTUCKY: GENETICS OR AN UNKNOWN CONDITION? 102

[82] SPONTANEOUS HUMAN COMBUSTION: SCIENTIFIC THEORIES AND NOTABLE CASES 103

[83] ANIMAL RAIN: FROM FISH TO SPIDERS 104

[84] MARFA LIGHTS: ATMOSPHERIC REFLECTIONS OR THE UNEXPLAINED? 105

CHAPTER TEN: MYSTICAL PLACES 107

[85] THE DEVIL'S SEA (DRAGON'S TRIANGLE): DISAPPEARANCES AND LEGENDS 108

[86] THE ZONE OF SILENCE: ANOMALIES AND STRANGE OCCURRENCES 109

[87] THE BENNINGTON TRIANGLE: ANALYZING MAJOR DISAPPEARANCES 110

[88] SKINWALKER RANCH: UFOS TO CRYPTIDS 111

[89] THE NEVADA TRIANGLE: THE BERMUDA TRIANGLE'S COUNTERPART 112

[90] HOIA-BACIU: THE HAUNTED ROMANIAN FOREST 113

[91] BRIDGEWATER TRIANGLE: A HUB OF PARANORMAL ACTIVITY 114

[92] MOUNT RORAIMA: LEGENDS OF A LOST WORLD .. 115

[93] AOKIGAHARA FOREST: THE DARK ALLURE OF JAPAN'S HAUNTED FOREST 116

CHAPTER ELEVEN: ENIGMATIC INDIVIDUALS 119

[94] D.B. COOPER: THE INFAMOUS SKYJACKER WHO VANISHED 120

[95] THE BABUSHKA LADY AT THE JFK ASSASSINATION: WHO WAS SHE? 121

[96] THE IDENTITY OF JACK THE RIPPER: A CENTURY-LONG MANHUNT 122

[97] THE ISDAL WOMAN: MULTIPLE FALSE IDENTITIES AND HER UNSOLVED DEATH 123

[98] KASPAR HAUSER: THE BOY WHO APPEARED FROM NOWHERE 124

[99] THE COUNT OF ST. GERMAIN: THE MAN WHO CLAIMED TO BE CENTURIES OLD 125

[100] THE LADY OF DAI: THE WELL-PRESERVED MUMMY WITH AN ENIGMATIC PAST 126

[101] LORI ERICA RUFF: THE WOMAN WITH TWO IDENTITIES 128

CONCLUSION 130

INTRODUCTION

Whether it's the ancient world or the modern day, there's no shortage of mysteries, conspiracies, and strange encounters throughout human history. Sightings of unusual creatures and unexplained phenomena have long baffled scientists, suggesting we still have much to learn about where we fit in the universe around us.

As you read *The Greatest Mysteries in History*, you'll discover conundrums and anomalies from dozens of different locations and time periods. From the Moai of Easter Island to the disappearance of D.B. Cooper, this book will lead you through some of the most perplexing events and archaeological artifacts. You'll even learn about unsolved ciphers and the stories behind some of the most dangerous places on the planet.

Entries for some of these mysteries include accompanying theories and opinions from experts in related fields. Remember to keep an open mind as you delve into the unexplained. Many of these bizarre sightings and events are rooted in forces we have yet to understand. A few may even be proof of paranormal activity or the existence of extraterrestrial life.

CHAPTER ONE:
COSMIC CONUNDRUMS

[1]
THE BLACK KNIGHT SATELLITE: ORIGINS AND TRACKING

In 1899, the famed Serbian-American scientist Nikola Tesla revealed that he had intercepted radio signals from extraterrestrial life while conducting communications experiments in his home lab. He believed the messages may have come from Mars. Other unusual signals were detected in 1928 by Jørgen Hals, a Norwegian amateur radio operator. These events led many people to speculate that aliens might have installed a satellite to communicate with Earth.

Interest in the Black Knight satellite continued to grow as evidence mounted. The US Navy detected the presence of an unidentified satellite in 1960 that was originally suspected to belong to the Soviet Union, a theory that was later disproven. Three years later, an astronaut named Gordon Cooper reportedly saw an unidentified object in space while working on Project Mercury.

In 1973, a Scottish author named Duncan Lunan began studying the transmissions Hals had discovered decades prior. He determined that the radio signals could belong to an alien probe orbiting the moon. With the moon serving as a shield between the satellite and Earth, it would have been able to avoid detection for up to 13,000 years.

This idea was supported by the work of Ron Bracewell, a professor at Stanford University who studied alien probes. Lunan also believed the satellite may have originated in the vicinity of the Epsilon Boötis star system.

When NASA released a photograph of a large object floating in space in 1998, some people speculated that it was actually a picture of the alien probe. NASA considered the object to be space debris, but the agency has never positively identified its exact origins.

[2]
UFO SIGHTINGS THROUGHOUT HISTORY: ROSWELL TO RENDLESAM FOREST

During the summer of 1947, a civilian pilot reported seeing flying saucers that were traveling at impossible speeds. There were hundreds of other sightings, but the most famous incident was when William "Mac" Brazel found unidentifiable wreckage on his ranch in New Mexico.

Brazel contacted Roswell Army Air Force Base. Representatives from the military retrieved the material and issued a press release stating they'd recovered a "flying disc." The military later retracted the statement and identified the object as an ordinary weather balloon, but their lack of proof was unconvincing.

In 1951, three professors from Texas Tech's science department spotted lights flying over them at a high speed. A freshman even took a picture that was published in magazines and newspapers. The military's investigation concluded that the phenomenon was caused by lights reflecting off birds, but the lights were in a semicircle pattern and moving too fast to be birds, according to eyewitness accounts.

People in Tehran, Iran, called authorities in 1976 after noticing a bright light. When an F-4 jet went to assess the area, the instruments malfunctioned. The same thing happened when a second jet was dispatched to replace the first, but the pilot also saw glowing objects. The official story blames a meteor shower and poor maintenance for the event.

In late 1980, military personnel stationed near London saw strange lights above Rendlesham Forest. One person claimed to have found some type of UFO in the forest, and others reported unusual radiation readings and damage to the surrounding trees. A lieutenant colonel even recorded his thoughts as he viewed the lights. The government denied any proof of extraterrestrial activity.

[3]
DARK MATTER AND DARK ENERGY: THE UNIVERSE'S UNSEEN FORCES

The vast majority of the known universe is made up of dark energy. This unseen force is related to how the universe expands, but its growth rate isn't consistent over time. Expansion slowed from the Big Bang until roughly 7 billion years ago, when it started accelerating again for unknown reasons.

Even the world's leading scientists can't explain why theories about gravity and quantum physics don't explain the presence of dark energy. All they know is that the universe will continue to expand, which could change what future generations are able to see out in space.

Dark matter is another perplexing aspect of astronomy. Normal matter, like planets and stars, is visible. However, they account for less than 5 percent of all mass. The rest is made up of dark matter, which can't be seen with the naked eye. Instead, astronomers study dark matter by seeing how light moves around it.

When it was first described in 1933 by the astronomer Fritz Zwicky, experts thought maybe dark matter was made up of hydrogen gas. In modern times, however, instruments are advanced enough to confirm that dark matter is something entirely different. Researchers continue to search for ways to measure and detect dark matter, but none have been successful thus far.

[4]
THE TUNGUSKA EVENT:
A MYSTERIOUS EXPLOSION IN SIBERIA

On June 30, 1908, a massive explosion over a remote area of modern-day Russia sent the world into a frenzy. The thermal blast traveled over 40 miles, and the night sky glowed all over Europe and Asia. Researchers estimate that the force of the explosion was equivalent to that of 20 million tons of TNT.

Despite widespread interest in discovering the cause, no one attempted to investigate until 19 years later. Leonid Kulik, an expert in meteorites, assembled a team to head out to Tunguska, where the explosion had taken place. They never reached the site and had to turn back because of the extreme weather conditions in Siberia.

Kulik returned in 1927 and successfully reached the area. When Kulik attempted to speak to the locals, they were hesitant to discuss the event, believing it was a curse by the god of thunder. Kulik was forced to conclude that his initial theory of a meteorite causing the explosion was incorrect since there was no crater from impact.

Years later, in 2004, a Russian scientist named Yuri Lavbin led another expedition to Tunguska. His team was able to determine that the object had come from the west before exploding. The team discovered a piece of metal believed to be from a UFO and several quartz slabs with symbols of unknown significance.

Lavbin asserted that the explosion was caused by an alien spacecraft intentionally colliding with a meteor to prevent it from decimating the planet Earth. He claims that the quartz slabs are part of the ship's control panel, but without another source to confirm, their origins remain a mystery.

[5]
THE PIONEER ANOMALY: UNEXPLAINED DEVIATIONS IN SPACECRAFT TRAJECTORIES

The Pioneer 10 spacecraft was launched in 1972 with the aim of studying distant planets. Pioneer 11 followed a year later. These unmanned research vessels were able to make detailed observations of Jupiter and Saturn before continuing deeper into the solar system. The spacecraft also contained messages about their origins in case they were detected by extraterrestrial life.

The Pioneer models were designed with spin stabilization to prevent them from veering off course, and both were equipped with advanced transceivers that could track their locations with extreme accuracy. That's why researchers at NASA's Jet Propulsion Laboratory were especially confused in 1980 when the Pioneer 10 and Pioneer 11 weren't keeping pace with their predicted speeds.

The vessels ended up being thousands of kilometers short of their expected progress. The deviations were so baffling to scientists that they even wondered if the current understanding of physics and gravitation was incorrect. Other theories suggested that dust or solar radiation could have caused unpredictable changes in the paths of the Pioneer spacecraft.

Viktor Toth and Slava Turyshev developed a theory that uneven heating had caused the Pioneers to slow. Although their work has been accepted as a valid explanation by many modern-day physicists and researchers, not everyone agrees that heat was truly the underlying cause. Some experts believe the truth has never come to light.

[6]
TABBY'S STAR:
A STAR'S MYSTERIOUS DIMMING PATTERN

The star, formally known as KIC 8462852, is one and a half times as large as the sun and located approximately 1,000 light-years away from Earth. Even though it's supposed to have the same level of brightness at all times, it started periodically dimming at unpredictable intervals.

KIC 8462852 was given the nickname "Tabby's star" after Professor Tabetha Boyajian began studying its unusual appearance in 2015. After analyzing the star, Boyajian discovered that the star's brightness had decreased by up to 22 percent.

Astronomers suggested that another object in space was blocking the light from reaching a point where it could be perceived by researchers on Earth. Some experts believed a group of planets was in the way, but that would have meant there were over two dozen planets moving in perfect alignment to generate the exact fluctuations in the light from Tabby's star.

Between March 2016 and the end of 2017, researchers gathered at Las Cumbres Observatory in California to study the star. The observatory consists of 21 different telescopes from all over the world that function together to track stars even as the sun rises and sets. The researchers' findings confirmed that the light from KIC 8462852 was still dimming and brightening, but they couldn't determine a definitive cause.

Boyajian and other scientists hope that advancements in telescope technology will yield more data about this star's mysterious behavior. In the meantime, KIC 8462852 remains the only known star of its kind.

[7]
THE SEARCH FOR PLANET NINE: BEYOND NEPTUNE'S ORBIT

In 2014, expert astronomers from the Gemini Observatory and the Carnegie Institution for Science theorized that the gravity source they detected beyond Neptune could actually be another planet the same size as Earth or larger. Because of its suspected location, the planet was nicknamed "Planet Nine."

Researchers estimated that Planet Nine would be located approximately 400 to 800 times the distance from the Earth to the sun. This would place Planet Nine somewhere within the Kuiper Belt, where smaller bodies like Pluto are located.

It's rare for astronomers to search for a specific object over such great distances. NASA and other prestigious organizations like the Harvard-Smithsonian Center for Astrophysics have searched for Planet Nine using the most advanced telescopes in existence.

Although other planets have been found in the region, none are consistent with the estimated size and location of Planet Nine. Even after scanning a large section of the area, experts were only 95 percent sure that Planet Nine wasn't in one of the locations they had already analyzed. The distance and unpredictability of deep space make these types of searches incredibly challenging.

Specialized teams of experts continue to search for Planet Nine, but some astronomers doubt it exists at all. Competing theories argue that Planet Nine could really be a black hole or misunderstood forces acting in a remote area of space.

[8]
FAST RADIO BURSTS:
UNEXPLAINED COSMIC SIGNALS

In 2007, an astronomer named Duncan Lorimer discovered short bursts of radio waves emitting from distant galaxies. Each fast radio burst, or FRB, lasts for only milliseconds at most. The intensity is so strong that astronomers believe black holes or other extremely powerful phenomena must be behind them.

Up until recently, experts thought FRBs were transient, meaning they wouldn't repeat from the same location. However, in 2016, astronomers realized that fast radio bursts could occur more than once. This changed how they investigated and searched for FRBs.

Four years later, scientists realized that a fast radio burst they'd previously studied had repeated itself two more times. They started to believe that all FRBs repeat to some extent, but instruments on Earth might not be sensitive enough to capture the faintest signals in the cycle.

The Canadian Hydrogen Intensity Mapping Experiment (CHIME) Collaboration further supported this idea when it identified an FRB that repeats in a predictable pattern. The FRB sends out bursts for four days before falling silent for 12 days.

To date, no one has unraveled the purpose of these emissions. One theory states that FRBs could be produced by the collapse of neutron stars. Another claims supernovae could be generating the bursts. Two Harvard professors even believe the FRBs could be part of an extraterrestrial communication system.

[9]
THEORIES ON MULTIVERSES: ARE THERE PARALLEL UNIVERSES?

After the Big Bang, the universe rapidly expanded in a concept known as *inflation*. Even though expansion stopped in our universe, scientists believe it continues indefinitely, creating other universes as it goes. Collectively, these universes form a multiverse, but that doesn't mean they have anything in common. Even basic physics could differ from one universe to the next.

Ongoing inflation could also explain why other civilizations haven't made contact with Earth. Due to the speed of expansion, universes would be spread so far apart that it would be impossible to travel between them without inventing a way to travel faster than the speed of light.

Scientists also point out that not all universes will have the right elements and physical laws to support life forms. If intelligent life only exists as a rarity, it's unlikely that any two civilizations will be extremely similar due to the number of variables involved.

Another theory of multiverses is rooted in quantum mechanics. Tiny particles in a wave function can exist in multiple possible states. When someone observes the wave function, it collapses to form one reality out of several. This suggests that reality is determined by "selecting" a single option from among a series of open-ended outcomes.

According to the many-worlds theory, the other outcomes occur in different realities. If Outcome A occurs in this version of reality, then Outcome B would take place in an alternate universe. Each universe would be separate yet interrelated.

CHAPTER TWO:
ANCIENT ANOMALIES

[10]
ADVANCED ANCIENT TECHNOLOGIES: THE BAGHDAD BATTERY AND ANTIKYTHERA MECHANISM

The Baghdad Battery could potentially be the world's first battery. The simple design consists of a clay pot with a copper core and an iron rod protruding through the opening at the top. Scientists estimate it dates back to approximately 224 to 650 CE.

It was discovered in the 1930s by archaeologist Wilhelm König, but the exact circumstances are murky at best. He may have found it during an excavation in Baghdad in 1936. Others claim König discovered the battery in the basement of the National Museum of Iraq in 1938.

Critics point out that König might have decided it was a battery based on the presence of two metals when similar jars were simply used to hold scrolls. However, a battery would have required an electrolyte solution to function properly, and tests performed on the Baghdad Battery revealed that it most likely contained either vinegar or wine.

Another example of advanced ancient technology is the Antikythera Mechanism. This device dates back to roughly 205 to 60 BCE. It was discovered in 1901 off the coast of a Greek island among the remnants of an ancient merchant ship.

Researchers credit the Antikythera Mechanism as being the first known analog computer. The ancient Greeks could use the device to predict where celestial bodies would be at a future point. The user calibrated the mechanism by aligning it with the current positions of the sun, moon, and planets.

These sophisticated inventions suggest that ancient civilizations were perhaps more advanced than historians realize. Other advanced devices may still be awaiting discovery in sites around the world.

[11]
THE SACSAYHUAMÁN WALLS: PRECISELY CARVED STONES

The ancient citadel Sacsayhuamán was built north of Cusco, Peru, a city that once served as the capital of the Inca Empire. Sacsayhuamán dates back to the fifteenth century and includes various types of homes, shrines, and towers. The construction of its stone walls is so unique that Spaniards who saw Sacsayhuamán believed supernatural forces must have been at work.

Rumors claim that over 20,000 men from the surrounding area mined stone and assembled the walls of Sacsayhuamán. The stones are fit together without any mortar and matched with such precision that even a piece of paper can't slide in between.

A Spanish historian who visited Sacsayhuamán during construction recorded his observations. He wrote that the men rotated to avoid overexertion, and any laborers who were sick were sent home and replaced. This allowed the workers to take great care in how they shaped and laid each stone.

After the Spanish attack on Cusco that lasted from May 1536 to March 1537, the Spanish settlers dismantled a substantial portion of Sacsayhuamán to build another city. The only stones remaining at the site in the present day were too large for the conquerors to move.

Modern-day researchers have attempted to replicate how the walls at Sacsayhuamán were built. They even carried out experiments at another archaeological site in Peru to test different methods of moving megalithic stones. Although they were able to fit stones closely together, none of their experiments matched the precision of Sacsayhuamán.

[12]
THE MOAI OF EASTER ISLAND: TRANSPORT THEORIES

The Moai of Easter Island are carved stone monoliths that date back as far as 1400 CE. They were believed to make the surrounding farmland fertile, so the ruling class commissioned over 900 statues.

Once statues were completed, the Moai were brought to sacred platforms called *ahus,* which stood about four feet tall. Some ahu even featured multiple Moai. After they were in place, carvers created eye sockets to house eyes made of stone and coral. The eyes awakened the power within the Moai.

The largest known statue on the island is nicknamed "El Gigante." It reaches a height of 71.93 feet and weighs up to 165 tons. By comparison, the smallest Moai is only 3.76 feet in height. Three statues even have extra art added to their exteriors. This proves that the statues weren't meant to be uniform.

The size and weight of the Moai raises the question of how people on the island moved the statues. The statues could have been placed sideways on sleds and moved slowly using logs to roll the platforms forward. It's also possible that the Moai were transported in an upright position. Some researchers even believe the carvers used wooden fulcrums.

Regardless of the method, transporting the statues was no easy task. In fact, only 32 percent of the Moai currently in existence ever made it to their final destination. Several statues lie just beyond the quarry, while up to 45 percent are still in the quarry itself.

[13]
THE ORIGINS OF THE SPHINX: WATER EROSION CONTROVERSY

The age of the Sphinx has been an ongoing mystery for many archaeologists and ancient historians. The structure shows signs of water erosion that don't exist on any nearby structure, making it challenging to determine when the Sphinx was first carved.

During the 1950s, a French Egyptologist hypothesized that since the Sphinx's body was eroded by water over time, it must have been built before historical periods with significant rainfall. The Egyptologist believed the Sphinx could be a link between the lost city of Atlantis and ancient Egypt.

In 1979, a second Egyptologist by the name of John Anthony West agreed with the theory and suggested the Sphinx could have been subjected to erosion when the Nile flooded between 15,000 and 10,000 BCE. West was intrigued by the idea that the Sphinx had been originally constructed by Atlanteans, who later taught their methods to the ancient Egyptians.

West consulted geologist Robert Schoch about his research. They traveled to Egypt in 1990 to examine the Sphinx in person. Although Schoch didn't discuss Atlantis specifically, he determined that the Sphinx could have been constructed as early as 9700 BCE, a timeline consistent with the existence of Atlantis.

If the Sphinx truly predates ancient Egypt, it would disrupt the modern understanding of the entire ancient world. Although no concrete evidence of a lost civilization has ever been discovered, the Sphinx could be the key to unraveling this centuries-long mystery.

[14]
GÖBEKLI TEPE: WORLD'S OLDEST TEMPLE OR ASTRONOMICAL OBSERVATORY?

In 1994, archaeologists began excavating a newly discovered site called Gobekli Tepe, the oldest known temple in the world. Göbekli Tepe was built approximately 12,000 years ago in southern Turkey. Yet even after decades of excavation, researchers are still unsure about the exact purpose of the temple—and whether it's really a temple at all.

Some researchers believe Göbekli Tepe was actually the world's first observatory. The people who lived in the surrounding area worshipped the star Sirius. It's possible that Göbekli Tepe was constructed to align with the star for religious purposes, making it both an observatory and a temple of sorts.

However, the core team conducting research at Göbekli Tepe isn't convinced since there's no way to determine the original alignment of many key features like pillars. Some portions of Göbekli Tepe have been moved or destroyed, making it impossible to confirm a relationship with the star Sirius.

Another theory that supports the idea of an observatory notes that carvings found within Göbekli Tepe appear to show a comet hitting the Earth. That suggests the people who constructed Göbekli Tepe found the event to be relevant to the overall purpose of the structure.

One way to confirm the purpose of Göbekli Tepe is to keep excavating and see whether any evidence indicates the presence of roofs. If the buildings were fully enclosed, it couldn't have functioned as an astronomical site.

[15]
THE DROPA STONES:
ANCIENT ALIEN ARTIFACTS?

The story of the Dropa Stones can't be verified, but rumors claim that Chinese archaeologists discovered proof of alien life in 1938. While exploring a series of caves, they found graves with small humanoid beings and cave art depicting strange beings in space. They went deeper into the caves and unearthed 716 discs with intricate engravings.

One of the leaders on the excavation brought the discs back to his university for further analysis. His work was later continued by Dr. Tsum Um Nui, a colleague who discovered the stones featured hieroglyphics that were only visible on a microscopic level. The discs dated back to approximately 12,000 BCE.

Dr. Nui deciphered the hieroglyphics and learned that the discs contained the story of an alien race called the Dropa. The aliens had crash-landed and retreated into the caves to avoid conflicts with the humans who lived nearby. Eventually, the two races formed a truce and lived together in peace.

None of the universities Dr. Nui consulted were interested in publishing his work. When he retired, the discs were sent to Russia. Soviet scientists analyzed the discs and found they were made of an unusual material. The discs later vanished without explanation.

In 1974, an engineer from Austria arranged to photograph two discs that belonged to a Chinese museum. When he arrived, the manager he'd spoken with was gone, and the discs had disappeared. None of the original discs have ever been recovered.

[16]
THE PIRI REIS MAP:
AN ANCIENT MYSTERY

A German scholar studying at the Topkapi Palace library in 1929 discovered an unusual detail in a map from the sixteenth century. The map dates back to 1513 when an Ottoman explorer known as Piri Reis decided to record various routes between harbors and other points of interest. A note attached to the map explained that Piri Reis had created the map by consulting charts and maps, including one from Christopher Columbus.

For its time, the map was remarkably accurate. It showed Europe, Africa, North America, and South America but failed to record some of the smaller islands in the Caribbean. It did include an island called Antillia that was only ever rumored to exist.

The most notable detail about the map is that it includes Antarctica, which wasn't officially discovered until roughly 300 years *after* Piri Reis drew his map. Additionally, the version of Antarctica on the Piri Reis map isn't covered in ice.

These discrepancies caused some people to reconsider when Antarctica was discovered and contemplate whether an older civilization existed that could have explored the world with such precision. There's even a theory that the Piri Reis map was created by aliens who were able to draw land masses while viewing the planet from space.

Only a third of the Piri Reis map survived into the twentieth century, so there's no way to assess whether there were any other islands, continents, or mysterious additions to the other sections of the map.

[17]
THE RONGORONGO SCRIPT OF EASTER ISLAND: UNDECIPHERED SYMBOLS

The Moai statues aren't the only mysteries from Easter Island. Historians have long wondered about the meaning of the rongorongo hieroglyphic script found on ancient wooden tablets. Only 24 artifacts featuring rongorongo symbols still exist, and linguists have been attempting to decode the hieroglyphs since they were first discovered in the nineteenth century.

Since societies throughout the region often used sacred chants and incantations, researchers believe the wooden tablets helped priests remember the order of their recitations. The hieroglyphics likely served as a type of reference to keep various chants in order.

The hieroglyphs depict trees, people, turtles, and figures who might be deities. Some experts believe the writing is based on concepts more than individual words, which would make it a form of pictographic communication. Similar markings appear in petrographs and rock art from different areas of Easter Island. To date, rongorongo is the only ancient script known to exist in Polynesia.

When the Bishop of Tahiti received one of the tablets in the mid-1800s, he attempted to find a local translator from among the Indigenous population. No one would tell him what the symbols meant. They either wouldn't share the truth with an outsider or didn't know how to interpret the symbols.

[18]
THE MYTHS OF EL DORADO: QUEST FOR THE CITY OF GOLD

Rumors of a city of gold began to circulate in Europe in the early sixteenth century. This drove Spanish kings to send their subjects throughout the region in search of riches and wealth. In reality, El Dorado was more likely a person rather than a place.

The Muisca people lived in modern-day Colombia from approximately 600 to 1600 CE. When a new king was crowned, they held a ritual where their new monarch was dusted with gold and brought to the center of a lake to offer tributes to the gods. The extravagance of the ceremony caused some Europeans to believe the Muisca were hiding an entire city of gold.

Famous explorers such as Sir Walter Raleigh launched expeditions to find El Dorado. The lake, which is known as Lake Guatavita, is actually the crater at the top of a volcano. In the 1580s, Antonio de Sepúlveda drained it to see if gold and tributes from coronation rituals had accumulated at the bottom. Although they found some golden items, the discovery was far from the famed riches of El Dorado.

In 1909, a British company called Contractor Limited attempted to drain the lake again. They managed to remove all the water, but the mud quickly hardened in the sunlight and was too durable to sort through by hand. The company went in search of heavy equipment to break apart the lakebed. By the time they returned, the tunnel they'd constructed to hold the water had failed, causing the lake to refill.

With modern technologies, archaeologists and researchers may yet discover new clues at the bottom of Lake Guatavita. By uncovering more artifacts from the time of Muisca kings, it's possible that dreams of a city of gold may yet come true.

CHAPTER THREE:
MYSTERIOUS CREATURES

[19]
EL CHUPACABRA:
ORIGINS AND DESCRIPTIONS

Rumors of a bloodsucking monster attacking animals in North and South America date back to the 1950s, but the story of the Chupacabra truly started to take root in 1995 after a series of unusual attacks against livestock in Puerto Rico. Residents and farmers all over the island found animals drained of blood with mysterious puncture wounds on their necks.

Before long, people began to wonder if there was a monster on the loose. Their fears only worsened after multiple eyewitness accounts described a creature with unnatural oval eyes, spikes on its back, and scaly skin. They named it *el chupacabra*, which translates to "goat sucker."

The Chupacabra is estimated to stand at roughly four to six feet tall when upright, giving it the ability to hunt both large and small prey. By the end of 1995, the chupacabra was believed to have killed over 1,000 animals. It attacked sheep, cattle, chickens, and even pets. One photograph from that time shows a cat with a fatal puncture wound straight through its skull.

Theories about the chupacabra vary widely. Some people claim it was left behind by extraterrestrials who visited Earth, while others think sightings could actually be coyotes with severe cases of mange. Although concrete evidence of the chupacabra has never been discovered, attacks from a bloodsucking creature have been recorded in multiple countries and cultures.

[20]
MERMAIDS AND MERMEN: SIGHTINGS AND MYTHS

Mermaids and mermen have the upper body of a human and the lower body of a fish. Stories of sirens — mermaids who lured sailors to their deaths with their songs — can be traced back thousands of years to ancient Assyria and Babylonia. The goddess Atargatis appeared as a mermaid. Mermen also appeared as deities in ancient Greece and Rome, most famously in the figure of Triton, son of Poseidon.

Throughout history, even cultures that didn't see mermaids and mermen as deities believed they had special powers. In Finland, mermen were said to be able to cure illnesses and craft magical potions. In Chinese folklore, mermaid tears could transform into pearls.

There are even mermaid sightings recorded in historical documents and publications. One of the most famous sightings took place in 1913 in the waters by Hoy, an island off the coast of Scotland. While searching for lobster, a fishing crew spotted a mermaid rising out of the water. Locals believed it was the Deerness Mermaid, a creature that had been seen hundreds of times in the surrounding areas at the end of the nineteenth century.

The mermaid in Hoy is particularly interesting because it matches the description of a merman from a medieval text. The description from Norse sailors says that the merman rose from the water and had a human body that narrowed from the shoulders down.

One theory claims that cold ocean water mixing with warmer air can create a vortex that distorts a person's vision at a distance. However, this doesn't explain why mermaids and mermen have also been spotted in areas that have warm or tropical waters.

[21]
THE JERSEY DEVIL:
HIDDEN IN THE PINE BARRENS

Before Europeans settled in modern-day New Jersey, the land was inhabited by the Lenni Lenape tribe. The Lenni Lenape knew that a spirit named Mising lived in the area, and they even had a ceremony in Mising's honor. One person would even dress up in costume to resemble the creature. Mising had horns, a long tail, and wings.

When the Europeans arrived, they built villages in the Pine Barrens, a part of New Jersey the Lenni Lenape had long avoided. Before long, people reported seeing a monster with horns and large eyes. It could fly or run along the ground, and it made a shrieking sound that could paralyze its prey.

Over time, the villagers in the Pine Barrens learned to take precautions with their livestock and young children. If pets went missing or a wildfire struck the area, they blamed it on the Jersey Devil. No one knew the full extent of its powers.

The attacks stopped throughout the nineteenth century, and local residents wondered if the creature was simply gone. But in the beginning of 1909, the Jersey Devil returned in force. The fear grew so pronounced that policemen and groups of armed men even tried to find and kill it, but they were unsuccessful.

After a nearly week-long onslaught of mischief and chaos, the Jersey Devil disappeared once more. People occasionally claim to see the Jersey Devil, but it has yet to emerge the way it did in 1909. It is said that if the monster goes dormant for lengthy periods of time, it may return with a vengeance in the years to come.

[22]
MOKELE-MBEMBE:
AFRICA'S MYTHICAL DINOSAUR?

The dinosaur-like creature known as Mokele-mbembe is said to reside in the vicinity of the Congo Basin in Central Africa. In addition to its enormous body, it's said to have a small head with a long neck and tail. Some people also claim that the Mokele-mbembe has a horn to protect itself and defend its territories along the water.

References to the Mokele-mbembe were pervasive among Indigenous peoples in the area, but Westerners weren't aware of the creature until 1776 when a French missionary found gigantic footprints measuring over three feet across. Another explorer wrote about the Mokele-mbembe in 1909, comparing it to a dinosaur.

Rumors state the Mokele-mbembe is an herbivore that loves to eat liana, a type of vine common throughout Africa. Based on its appearance and diet, one theory is the Mokele-mbembe is actually a dinosaur that survived from prehistoric times. The survival of one dinosaur also suggests there are others of the same species that have continued to live in remote parts of Africa and reproduce.

Those who doubt the existence of the Mokele-mbembe point out that no evidence of modern-day dinosaurs has ever been found in the area. None of the investigations throughout the region have yielded bones, feces, or other traces of the creature. However, given the dense nature of the forest and how little some areas have been explored, it's possible that even an animal the size of the Mokele-mbembe could evade detection.

[23]
THUNDERBIRDS:
GIANT BIRDS OF NATIVE AMERICAN
LORE

When the first European colonists were arriving in North America, the Indigenous peoples shared stories of a great bird that could call thunder just by beating its wings. It was said that thunderbirds brought rain to help plants grow and protected Indigenous tribes from evil forces.

Skeptics claim that Native Americans most likely mistook large birds of prey as thunderbirds, but historical accounts describe thunderbirds as having a wingspan of up to 23 feet. Since even condors only have wingspans of 10.5 feet, it seems unlikely that anyone could mix up birds with such strikingly different proportions.

Furthermore, the existence of an enormous bird is possible from a scientific standpoint. Indigenous tribes believed the thunderbirds resided high in the mountains, which would be the most appropriate habitat for a species of that size. In the open and remote areas that once existed in North America, there would be abundant prey to support larger predators.

From a cultural perspective, it's also important to consider that Native American tribes worshipped many real animals, such as cougars. Therefore, the thunderbird may have existed in earlier times before human population growth made it more challenging for them to survive.

In 2018, a woman in Alaska reported seeing a bird of roughly the same size as a thunderbird. This suggests that thunderbirds may still exist in the few open territories remaining in North America.

[24]
YOWIE AND YETI:
BIGFOOT'S INTERNATIONAL COUSINS

Bigfoot was first referenced in a 1958 newspaper article describing strange footprints found by loggers in northern California. Over time, this evolved into an enduring myth throughout America. However, other parts of the world also have their own legends about mysterious creatures that walk on two legs.

The Australian version of Bigfoot is an ape-like creature named Yowie that lives in the wilderness. It's said to stand up to 12 feet tall and have feet that are far larger than any human's. Similarly, the Yeti is rumored to live in the Himalayan mountains between Nepal and Tibet. The descriptions of the Yeti are more varied, and some cultures believe there are several types with different features.

There are even some experts who believe in the existence of a creature like Bigfoot or its international cousins. Jeff Meldrum, an Idaho State University professor of anthropology, has collaborated with a forensic specialist to analyze casts of unusual footprints. The forensic scientist concluded one footprint found in Washington State in 1987 is especially authentic since it features a completely new print pattern and ridges that correspond to extremely thick skin.

There's also the Skookum Cast, a plaster cast taken from the impression of an unidentifiable animal made in the mud after lying down. Meldrum believes it was made by a primate up to 50 percent larger than humans. Even Jane Goodall, the researcher famed for her work with chimpanzees, believes a creature like Bigfoot could exist.

[25]
GIGANTIC SEA SERPENTS: REPORTS AND MYTHS

Myths of gigantic sea serpents are pervasive throughout the world. The famous Hydra from ancient Greek mythology grew two heads for every one that was cut off, making it nearly impossible to kill. In ancient Japanese lore, Ryujin was a sea dragon with the power to control the tides.

But there are also historical accounts from people who have claimed to see real serpents in the open ocean. In 1638, a man named John Josselyn reported a sea serpent in the vicinity of Cape Ann, Massachusetts. A similar serpent was spotted in nearby Gloucester in the early nineteenth century.

In 1848, sailors on the HMS *Daedalus* saw a sea serpent swimming nearby while traveling off the west coast of southern Africa. According to the captain, the creature's head extended a full four feet above the surface of the ocean.

Skeptics believe witnesses confused sea serpents with other species. Giant oarfish, for instance, have a snake-like appearance and can grow up to 36 feet in length. A giant oarfish could easily be confused with a mythical monster under the right conditions.

On the other hand, only a small portion of the world's oceans have been explored. There are countless unknown species that have yet to be discovered. Other gigantic creatures like the megalodon once existed, so it's possible that the sea serpents in historical accounts are real as well.

[26]
MOTHMAN:
THE MYSTERY

In late 1966, two couples claimed to have encountered a monster on the highway by Point Pleasant, West Virginia. It chased them on foot but was unable to keep up until it took to the skies. The four witnesses went to the police and reported seeing a human-like creature with massive wings and eyes that glowed red. The newspaper dubbed this strange being "Mothman."

Before long, others claimed to have seen Mothman outside their homes or in the woods. A local man named Newell Partridge even came forward stating Mothman had appeared by his home in nearby Salem, West Virginia, the night before the couples saw the creature on the highway. Patridge's dog had run away, chasing after two red circles glowing in the darkness. When he followed the paw prints, they went in circles and then abruptly stopped.

No one knows the true origins of Mothman. Some people speculate that Mothman was created by radiation from West Virginia factories that made explosives during World War II. The town where Mothman first appeared was home to one such factory. Thus far, there aren't any clues about why Mothman disappeared or what might have drawn it away from Point Pleasant.

Mothman sightings in Point Pleasant ended in 1967 after a fatal bridge collapse claimed the lives of 40 people. Witnesses wondered whether there was a connection to Mothman. After that, rumors of a moth-like monster could be heard all throughout the United States. One researcher even believes the Mothman legend made its way to Russia. The most recent sighting of a creature resembling Mothman was in Chicago in 2019.

[27]
THE LOVELAND FROG: HIDDEN IN OHIO

The story of the Loveland Frog is somewhat controversial. There are several different accounts of the first time the frog was seen. This could mean that multiple sightings were combined as the story was passed down over the years, or maybe some locals were just unclear on the exact details of what occurred back in 1955.

In the first version, a traveling salesman was driving along an empty road near Loveland, Ohio, when he spotted three figures standing in the road. He honked his horn, but when they turned to look at him, the man saw strange skin and faces that resembled a frog's. They were approximately four feet tall and could stand on their hind legs.

Another story claims the motorist actually saw them under a bridge spanning the Little Miami River. One of the frogs leaped onto the hood, and the salesman was so shocked that he passed out. Others even claim that the frogs under the bridge were capable of doing magic and had wands that could shoot sparks.

In 1972, a police officer named Ray Shockey reported seeing the Loveland Frog as it ran in front of his vehicle. Another officer later saw a large iguana with a missing tail in the same area and shot it as proof that his colleague had been mistaken about seeing the frog. Although Shockey agreed at the time that his eyes had deceived him, he continued to tell the story of how he encountered the Lakeland Frog.

In the summer of 2016, two teenagers playing near Lake Isabella saw a frog that stood up on its hind legs and walked. The creature matched the description of what the salesman had seen all those years before in 1955, suggesting that maybe the Loveland Frog had returned.

[28]
LAKE MONSTERS AROUND THE WORLD: CHAMP, OGOPOGO, AND MORE

From Uganda to Iceland, there are stories of strange creatures residing in the world's deepest lakes. Some people believe these large beasts have survived in secret since prehistoric times, while others claim they're truly monsters that stretch the bounds of reality.

One of the most famous lake monsters is Champ, a dinosaur-like creature rumored to live in Lake Champlain along the border of New York and Vermont. Locals believed Samuel de Champlain himself wrote about seeing Champ in the lake until his journals were translated at the end of the nineteenth century.

He actually documented seeing a particular breed of fish rather than the famous lake monster, but that hasn't stopped hundreds of others from spotting Champ over the years. In 2003, researchers recorded sounds from within Lake Champlain that were consistent with whales and dolphins, but neither resided in the lake.

The Ogopogo lake monster in British Columbia's Okanagan Lake is described as a serpentine creature with dark skin and multiple humps. Interest in Ogopogo grew to such heights in the 1980s that the regional tourism association offered $1 million to anyone who could provide definitive proof of Ogopogo's existence.

In the Democratic Republic of Congo and Uganda, the irizima is said to reside in Lake Edward. According to Captain William Hichens, the first to discuss the monster, he heard that the irizima has the appearance of a massive hippopotamus with horns and lizard's head. A hunter who claimed to see the irizima noted that it created waterspouts in Lake Edward.

CHAPTER FOUR: DISAPPEARING ACTS

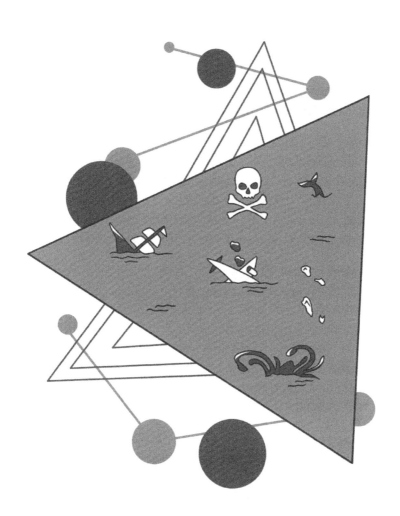

[29]
THE BERMUDA TRIANGLE: HISTORICAL DISAPPEARANCES AND THEORIES

The Bermuda Triangle is the area of the Atlantic Ocean formed by drawing straight lines between Bermuda, Miami, Florida, and San Juan, Puerto Rico. It encompasses up to 1.5 million square miles. Over the years, dozens of ships and multiple aircraft have disappeared without a trace.

On February 22, 1918, the USS *Cyclops* departed Salvador, Brazil, with a destination of Baltimore, Maryland. It made an unscheduled stop in Barbados to check the integrity of the ship before continuing on March 4, 1918. The ship was transporting 10,800 long tons of manganese ore and had 306 people aboard when it disappeared somewhere in the Bermuda Triangle.

Decades later, in late 1945, a set of five Avenger torpedo bombers called Flight 19 were conducting training exercises off the coast of Florida when they got lost. Lieutenant Charles C. Taylor believed his instruments were malfunctioning and started flying northeast rather than heading west as protocol dictated. When their transmissions cut out, the Navy sent a pair of Martin PBM Mariners to search for them. Despite their enormous size, both of those planes vanished as well.

Not all disappearances occurred in the open ocean. In December 1967, a luxury cruiser named the *Witchcraft* called for aid from a mile offshore after striking an object in the water. The boat's owner stated it wasn't dire and said he would light a flare to show their location. Rescuers arrived within 20 minutes but found no sign of a boat. The owner and his guest were never found.

Although the Bermuda Triangle is said to be home to supernatural forces, the prevailing scientific theory is that extreme weather has caused most of these disappearances. There's also evidence to suggest that compasses redirect to true north rather than magnetic north, further complicating the task of navigating through the area.

[30]
FLIGHT MH370:
THE SEQUENCE OF EVENTS AND INVESTIGATION

On March 8, 2014, flight MH370 departed Kuala Lumpur for an overnight flight with a final destination of Beijing, China. The jet was piloted by Zaharie Ahmad Shah, one of the airline's most seasoned and experienced pilots. Most of the passengers were Chinese or Malaysian, but there were also citizens from a dozen other nations onboard.

At 1:19 a.m., MH370 signed off with Malaysian air traffic controllers as they were nearing Vietnamese airspace but never made contact with controllers in Ho Chin Minh as planned. Mere moments after entering the skies over Vietnam, the flight disappeared from all radar and failed to respond to communications.

Only one satellite had any connection with MH370 over the next few hours. It briefly connected seven times, indicating that MH370 had turned around sharply and continued out over the Indian Ocean until it ran out of fuel. The plane likely crashed west of Australia. Debris was recovered by the coasts of Mozambique and Madagascar, but there were no conclusive links to MH370.

The prevailing theory is that Zaharie crashed the plane as part of a sophisticated murder-suicide. The flight simulator data from his home contained a path that somewhat resembled the actual route of MH370. Other analysts believe the plane was either hijacked by Russian operatives to distract the world from the Russian invasion of the Crimean Peninsula or deliberately shot down by the United States to prevent unknown cargo from falling into Chinese hands.

Unfortunately, this long after the event, it's unlikely that any material evidence from the crash will surface. The real question is whether further investigation will reveal the involvement of a military force or organized group with political motives.

[31]
THE ROANOKE COLONY: THEORIES AND CLUES LEFT BEHIND

Sir Walter Raleigh established the first English colony in the New World in 1585 at Roanoke, an island off the coast of modern-day North Carolina. The settlers struggled to find enough to eat, and the Indigenous tribes often launched attacks against the colonists. They returned to England a year later and were replaced with a second group of approximately 115 people.

The second set of colonists were also unprepared. The governor, John White, returned to England to ask for more support but wasn't able to return for three years because of the war with Spain. When White arrived back in Roanoke in 1590, the colonists had vanished.

The only clue left behind was the word *Croatoan* carved into a tree. This seemed to indicate the colonists had relocated to nearby Croatoan Island, now known as Hatteras Island, but White was unable to find them there either. Roanoke came to be known as the "Lost Colony."

There are many theories about what really happened to the settlers. They could have been killed by natural causes like drought or disease. It's also possible they died out after an attack by Native Americans or Spanish ships.

Some historians believe the colonists survived by assimilating into nearby Indigenous tribes. This claim is supported by pottery shards that were found close to a Native American settlement on the mainland. However, those artifacts could also have belonged to other settlers from colonies like Jamestown, which was founded in 1607.

Future archaeological discoveries may yield more clues about what happened to the Roanoke settlers. With technological advances like ground-penetrating radar, it's easier than ever to find sites that were previously lost to history.

[32]
THE SODDER CHILDREN DISAPPEARANCE: A FAMILY'S RELENTLESS SEARCH

In the early morning hours of Christmas Day in 1945, a fire destroyed the Fayetteville, West Virginia, home of George and Jennie Sodder. Four of their children made it outside, but when they went to rescue the remaining five from the upper floors, the ladder they kept outside was nowhere to be found.

Unable to reach the children, they attempted to call the fire department only to realize the phone line wouldn't connect. By the time any help arrived, flames had consumed the entire house. The fire inspector believed the blaze had been caused by faulty wiring and claimed that the heat had eliminated any trace of human remains inside.

The Sodders were suspicious since household items were found in the ashes. They also recalled several unusual details leading up to Christmas Day. On multiple occasions, people had referenced fire or the wiring in the home, which could have been veiled threats against George for speaking out against Mussolini in an area where many Italian immigrants still supported him.

An investigator hired by the Sodders later discovered that one of the people who'd threatened the Sodders was involved in ruling the fire accidental. The fire chief also confessed to hiding a beef liver at the scene in an attempt to convince the family it was a human heart and get them to call off the search for survivors.

Many eyewitnesses claimed to have seen the children leaving the scene or in the surrounding area. George and Jennie continued to follow every lead. In 1968, they received a mysterious photo claiming to depict their son Louis. They never identified the sender or successfully tracked down any of the five children. Even after their deaths, their descendants have continued their search for the truth.

[33]
THE FLANNAN ISLES LIGHTHOUSE KEEPERS: ABANDONED IN A STORM?

On December 15, 1900, a ship called the *Archtor* passed by the Flannan Isles Lighthouse off the coast of Scotland and noticed the light was out. A week and a half later, a relief vessel for the lighthouse arrived at the location and found it empty. The three lighthouse keepers—Thomas Marshall, James Ducat, and Donald MacArthur—were missing.

The crew of the relief vessel found everything mostly in order. The lighthouse had been properly maintained, and the interior was in an orderly condition. On the outside, however, there were broken railings and signs of a severe storm.

The logbook from the lighthouse contained notes up until December 15, suggesting the storm must have struck in between making those records and the arrival of the *Archtor*. While investigating, the crew also noted that the clock had stopped working, and one of the lighthouse keepers had left without his coat.

Several years later, a logbook that supposedly belonged to the Flannan Isles Lighthouse surfaced. There were bizarre notes from December 12 through December 15. The records indicated that a storm was coming and described strange behaviors by the lighthouse keepers. The authenticity of the logbook couldn't be verified.

It's possible the men had been in a hurry to secure equipment when they were caught up in a wave and swept out to sea. Others speculated that MacArthur, who was rumored to have a violent past, killed Ducat and Marshall before committing suicide. Despite ongoing interest in the story of the Flannan Isles Lighthouse, the disappearance of the three lighthouse keepers has never been solved.

[34]
THE ANGIKUNI LAKE DISAPPEARANCE: AN ENTIRE VILLAGE VANISHES

In 1930, a hunter named Joe Labelle, traveling through a remote region of Nunavut, decided to seek out a place to spend the night. The Inuit people maintained a fishing village along Angikuni Lake, so he headed there to find lodging. But when he arrived, the village was deserted in the eeriest of ways.

Labelle found half-eaten meals and sled dogs that had starved to death. Since the Inuit worked and lived closely with their dogs, they never would have willingly left them behind. However, Labelle couldn't find any signs of a struggle or evidence that the residents had fled from an attack. It looked as though the people who lived there had simply vanished into thin air.

He was even more disturbed when he noticed that a grave on the outskirts of the village had been dug up, the damage too neat to have been an animal. Labelle went to the police and explained the situation. The police analyzed the scenes at the village and guessed that the villagers had been missing for approximately two months.

While they were searching for clues, officers noticed unusual lights in the sky over Angikuni Lake. People started to speculate that maybe the missing villagers had been abducted by aliens. No survivors from the region were ever found, and the police eventually decided to close the case as a hoax made up by Labelle.

[35]
FREDERICK VALENTICH: A PILOT'S UNEXPLAINED MID-FLIGHT DISAPPEARANCE

The disappearance of 20-year-old Frederick Valentich is both a cold case and a potential encounter with extraterrestrial life. On October 21, 1978, Valentich departed from Melbourne, Australia, in his single-engine plane. He was planning to fly to nearby King Island to pick up some friends.

But once he was over the ocean, he contacted air traffic controllers to report a strange aircraft that had appeared by his Cessna 182. No other planes were supposed to be in the area, so Valentich described what he could tell about its appearance. He stated it was long, moving quickly, and emitting green light. Valentich was convinced it was a UFO.

Suddenly, the object vanished and reappeared from a different angle. Valentich's communications began to break up as he informed air traffic controllers that his plane was experiencing mechanical problems. His last transmission was sent just after 7 p.m. before the channel went silent.

Within half an hour, the official search began when Valentich failed to land at King Island as intended. Rescue crews spent five days looking for any sign of Valentich or his aircraft, but nothing was ever found. Even the plane's emergency beacon had seemingly vanished.

Flying is inherently dangerous and unpredictable, but Valentich was flying an easy journey with clear skies and no known storms. Until he saw the UFO, he never mentioned any issues with his engine. It was only after the UFO returned to hover above him that Valentich noticed his aircraft beginning to falter.

[36]
THE MISSING NINTH LEGION OF ROME: A LEGION LOST TO HISTORY

The Ninth Legion was established in 65 BCE, and it was one of the four legions Julius Caesar took with him to conquer Gaul. The legion later fought in Egypt against Cleopatra and Mark Antony before relocating in 43 CE to support the Roman invasion of Britain.

After moving north in a series of battles, the Ninth came under the command of Gnaeus Julius Agricola in a region that encompasses modern-day Scotland. Part of Agricola's strategy was to divide his forces into smaller units. Their enemy, the Caledonians, learned of his plan and launched an attack against the Ninth while it was vulnerable.

The Caledonians had the advantage, and the situation was bleak for the Ninth Legion. Agricola arrived just in time to trap and defeat them. After their campaign with Agricola, the Ninth was stationed at Eboracum until at least the year 108 CE.

On a list of all legions dating back to 165 CE, the Ninth was notably missing. No one knows what happened to the legion in the intervening years. Some historians believe the Ninth was defeated in an attack on Eboracum, while others theorize that the legion was destroyed while trying to quell an uprising in the north in 118 CE.

It's also possible the Ninth was simply transferred out of Britain as the region became increasingly hostile to the Romans. In approximately 125 CE, researchers found artifacts in the Rhine that bore the mark of the Ninth. This could have been a smaller detachment that separated from the group in Britain or the location of the Ninth's reassignment after the legion departed Eboracum.

[37]
THE COPPER SCROLL:
A LOST TREASURE

The Dead Sea Scrolls were first discovered in 1947 in the Qumran Caves of the West Bank. The scrolls are written primarily in Hebrew, with languages such as Greek, Aramaic, and Latin appearing in some manuscripts. Most of them are made of parchment or papyrus, but one in particular stuck out for its unusual material — copper.

The Copper Scroll was found in Cave 3 on March 14, 1952. Because of wear on the metal, the scroll couldn't be opened, so it was transported to Manchester University in the UK to be cut into separate pieces. This allowed researchers to read the scroll.

While most other Dead Sea Scrolls contained religious texts or hymns, the Copper Scroll lists 64 locations where tons of precious metals are hidden. Each entry explains the general region, the specific site, and how far down the items are buried.

John Allegro, an expert on the Dead Sea Scrolls, visited each site in 1962 to search for artifacts. His team was unable to find any signs of treasure. It's possible, however, that the instructions weren't specific enough to pinpoint an area in modern times without fully understanding all the ancient locations and references.

Some historians have claimed the treasures described in the Copper Scroll aren't real, but it's far more likely that the items were found long ago during ancient times. The Romans actively sought to find hidden valuables after invading a new area so they could have learned of the existence of the Copper Scroll. It's also possible the people who originally made the scroll recovered the treasure.

[38]
THE VANISHING OF PERCY FAWCETT: AN EXPLORER'S QUEST FOR THE CITY OF Z

Percy Fawcett was a British explorer and a lieutenant colonel who served in World War I. After spending years in South America mapping boundaries and drawing borders for the Royal Geographical Society, he was determined to find the "lost city of Z," an advanced civilization reminiscent of El Dorado.

Fawcett's belief in a lost city was partially based on observations by a group of explorers from Portugal who claimed to have found ancient ruins in 1753. They recorded their findings in a document known as Manuscript 512. Fawcett thought the presence of another civilization supported his theories about the city of Z.

In early 1925, Fawcett set out into the jungle with his son Jack and a friend. They traveled for several months, sending letters to their loved ones back home and updating the world on their progress. As a seasoned explorer who was intimately familiar with the region, Fawcett had long held a reputation for surviving in the inhospitable jungles of South America. But after May 29, no one heard from the expedition again.

The prevailing theory is that Fawcett, his son, and their traveling companion were all killed by hostile Indigenous tribes. According to later interviews with the Kalapalo people, the tribe last saw them heading into dangerous territory.

Fawcett's wife, Nina, was convinced they would return, but the fate of the three men remains unknown to this day. Since Fawcett's disappearance, up to 100 people have died searching for clues about Fawcett's disappearance near the Xingu River in Brazil.

CHAPTER FIVE:
CRYPTIC CODES AND
LANGUAGES

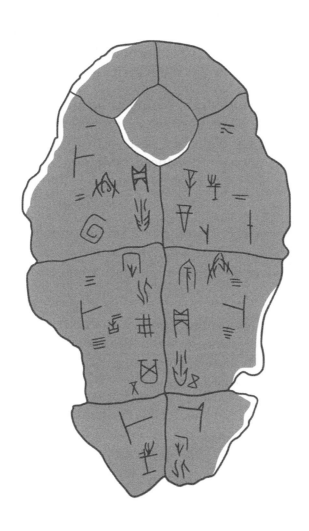

[39]
THE VOYNICH MANUSCRIPT: ORIGINS AND PURPOSE

Countless historians and linguists have sought to understand the Voynich manuscript, a mysterious book written in code during the fifteenth century. The manuscript changed hands several times until it was eventually purchased by the Holy Roman Emperor Rudolf II. It's now part of the collection at the Beinecke Rare Book & Manuscript Library at Yale University.

At over 200 pages in length, the manuscript contains numerous illustrations and appears to cover topics ranging from astronomy to botany. There may even be a section that contains recipes. All notes and drawings were produced by hand. Since the pages are numbered, it appears the book is incomplete and missing several pages.

The code itself consists of roughly 25 repeating characters, along with a handful that only appear in isolated instances. Historians have yet to discover any discernible form of punctuation to divide the text into sentences.

Detractors have claimed the Voynich manuscript is an elaborate hoax, but expert linguists agree that the code used in the book has patterns consistent with a real language. Radiocarbon dating of the vellum also proves its age is authentic.

Some historians believe the book is a medical guide due to its references to anatomy and plants. Other theories suggest the text is related to witchcraft. No one can know for sure until the manuscript is decoded.

Unfortunately, even famous cryptologists have been stumped by the manuscript. Elizebeth and William Friedman, the renowned American codebreakers from WWII, were similarly perplexed. As technology advances, supercomputers are trying their hand at deciphering the code, but none have been successful thus far.

[40]
THE ZODIAC KILLER'S CYPHERS: PARTIALLY SOLVED MESSAGES

The Zodiac Killer was an infamous serial killer who struck in Northern California in the late 1960s and early 1970s. He definitively killed at least five people and attacked two more, but he claimed to have been responsible for dozens of murders.

Unlike criminals who avoid police attention at all costs, the Zodiac Killer deliberately taunted both law enforcement and the media by sending them cryptic messages. His notes all started with the same phrase: *This is the Zodiac speaking.*

Toward the end of 1969, the Zodiac Killer sent a cipher to the *San Francisco Chronicle*. It came to be known as the 340 Cipher because it contained 340 characters. It would remain unsolved until December 2020, when a team of amateur codebreakers finally decoded it.

It all started when web designer David Oranchak created online videos about the cipher after being interested in the case for over a decade. An Australian mathematician named Dr. Samuel Blake used Oranchak's videos as a springboard to determine there were roughly 650,000 possible solutions.

From there, a Belgian warehouse operator named Jarl Van Eycke wrote a software tool to analyze the cipher. Contrary to claims made by the Zodiac Killer, there's no overt reference to his identity in the cipher. The message explains that the Zodiac Killer wasn't afraid of death because he had enough slaves to work for him in "paradice," a misspelling that repeats multiple times.

Many independent investigators believe the late Gary Francis Poste was the Zodiac Killer. Poste was rumored to be violent, and his features matched descriptions from the few survivors of Zodiac Killer attacks. Prior to his death, Poste gave away a large amount of ammunition and weaponry. However, the FBI is adamant that the case remains open and unsolved.

[41]
KRYPTOS: THE UNSOLVED SCULPTURE AT CIA HEADQUARTERS

The *Kryptos* sculpture was created by James Sanborn and installed at Langley, Virginia, at the headquarters of the US Central Intelligence Agency in 1990. It depicts a 12-foot copper scroll unfurling from around a petrified tree, but it's far from just decorative. The scroll consists of four panels with close to 1,800 characters that form several encrypted messages.

The coding scheme itself was developed by Ed M. Scheidt, a codes expert who collaborated with Sanborn. The two men were so secretive during the process that Sanborn had to memorize key details about how to create an encoded message, resulting in a few minor mistakes when he physically engraved the characters on the panels.

Three of the puzzles have been solved, but the meaning of the fourth has remained a mystery all these years. That's unsurprising to Scheidt since only the fourth panel was designed to present a true challenge. Scheidt never used his insider knowledge to uncover what Sanborn put on the fourth panel, so Sanborn is the only one who knows what *Kryptos* really says.

Sanborn has given the public multiple hints over the years by decoding single words at a time. He also disclosed that the first three panels contain clues to solving the fourth. But after keeping the secret for decades, Sanborn has considered auctioning off the solution to the last panel. This way, the mystery would live on if the cipher remained unsolved at the time of Sanborn's eventual death.

[42]
THE PHAISTOS DISK:
A MINOAN MYSTERY

Italian archaeologists uncovered the Phaistos Disk in the summer of 1908 during an excavation in the southern region of Crete. The disk is made of fired clay and measures approximately 5.9 inches across. Experts estimate that it was made between 1850 and 1550 BCE.

The Phaistos Disk contains 242 symbols when counting both sides, but only 45 symbols are unique. The symbols predominantly include cattle, flowers, and other references to nature, but humans and boats also appear in multiple places.

Unlike other artifacts from this time period, the disk was marked with individual stamps. Some symbols were also erased and stamped over. This suggests the use of moveable type and the intent to make the process of writing more efficient. In spite of this design, no other disks have ever been found.

Linguists have spent decades attempting to solve the mystery of the Phaistos Disk, but they can't even agree on the writing system. Researchers believe there are too many distinct symbols to make up a functional alphabet, but there aren't enough symbols for a pictographic system that would need to represent a variety of concepts. The last option is that each symbol stands for a single syllable.

One theory states that copies of the disk could have been sent to multiple locations to settle a dispute between leaders of different regions. That need for multiple identical disks would explain why the stamps were necessary. However, there simply aren't enough sources in the language to decipher the true meaning of the Phaistos Disk.

[43]
LINEAR A:
THE UNDECIPHERED MINOAN SCRIPT

Linear A is a type of script that was used by the Minoans from approximately 1850 to 1450 BCE. Since the Minoan civilization was based in Crete, clay tablets with Linear A have been discovered throughout the region. Linear A has never been deciphered, and neither has its predecessor, the Cretan Hieroglyphic script.

In some locations, both written languages were used for a brief overlapping period. However, as independent territories on Crete formed a more centralized society, the need grew for a uniform script that could be used widely across the island.

Although there's still much to learn about Linear A, historians believe it has at least 90 different characters that can be used to represent complex ideas like fractions. Thus far, researchers have identified up to 800 different words from analyzing the script.

In 2019, archaeologist Brent Davis of the University of Melbourne delivered a talk describing a new approach to studying undeciphered scripts from the Bronze Age. Instead of looking at each script in isolation, Davis theorized that comparing them to each other could yield new findings.

By analyzing Linear A script and the Phaistos Disk at the same time, Davis discovered enough overlapping commonalities to suggest they might represent the same language. Comparing scripts also revealed that a later script called Linear B has roughly 70% of the symbols that appear in Linear A. Linear B was deciphered relatively recently in 1952, recording an early version of the Greek language.

[44]
THE TAMÁM SHUD CASE: A MAN, A CODE, AND AN UNSOLVED DEATH

On the morning of December 1, 1948, pedestrians found a dead man lying on Somerton Beach in Adelaide, South Australia. He was roughly 40 years old and had clearly been in excellent physical shape. His cause of death was heart failure from possible poisoning.

The man was dressed in a suit and tie, but all the labels had been removed except for three that said *Keane*. Investigators also found a tiny piece of paper rolled up in a hidden pocket. The paper only contained the words *tamám shud*, which translates to "finished" in Persian. The authorities eventually determined the paper was cut from a copy of *The Rubaiyat*, a book of poetry by Omar Khayyam.

The police publicized the book and asked if anyone knew of a copy of *The Rubaiyat* with the final page removed. A man came forward with a copy that someone had placed in the back seat of his car while it was parked on the street. The back cover also had five lines of letters that might have been a type of code.

Speculation grew that perhaps the Somerton man was a spy of some sort. The next break in the case wouldn't come until 2022, when researchers identified a DNA match in a database. They slowly narrowed down the family tree until they found someone whose records matched the description of the man found on Somerton Beach.

Finally, they settled on Carl "Charles" Webb, an electrical engineer who lived in Melbourne and had no date of death listed. Carolyn Bilsborow, who directed a documentary about the case, speculated that Webb may have committed suicide.

[45]
THE D' AGAPEYEFF CIPHER: AN UNSOLVED CRYPTOGRAM

In 1939, a writer named Alexander D'Agapeyeff published a book called *Codes and Ciphers*. It detailed the history of cryptography and outlined several of the techniques used to create, analyze, and decode ciphers. At the end, D'Agapeyeff included a practice cipher that has remained unsolved for over 80 years.

This fact is notable on its own, but it's even more interesting because D'Agapeyeff was not a professional cryptologist. His publisher was interested in releasing a book on the subject, so D'Agapeyeff taught himself the key concepts. Unfortunately, he forgot how to decode his own cipher.

Most people agree on organizing the 395 digits in another orientation. In its original form, the digits are arranged in groups of five. Once those larger sets are split into pairs, it becomes easier to see a potential pattern. From there, cryptographers usually put the pairs into a 14 x 14 grid. This type of grid pattern breaks apart areas with repeating pairs since it's highly unlikely for any word to have the same letter appear three times.

It's possible that the key to decoding the cipher is based on a Polybius square, an encryption technique involving a 5 x 5 grid. The letters of a key word and the remaining letters of the alphabet are placed in each square. One square will have two letters to accommodate the 26 letters of the English alphabet. If placed in order, grid space 1 x 1 would be equivalent to the letter *A*.

Some cryptography hobbyists have also questioned whether the cipher uses words in another language. That might explain why it's remained unsolved for such an unusual length of time. Although *Codes and Ciphers* was written decades ago, the ongoing mystery of the unsolved cipher makes it relevant even in the present day.

[46]
THE RICKY MCCORMICK NOTES: ENCRYPTED MESSAGES OR GIBBERISH?

Ricky McCormick's body was found in a cornfield in West Alton, Missouri, on June 30, 1999. Since McCormick didn't own a vehicle, investigators weren't sure how he'd ended up approximately 15 miles away from home. When they searched his pockets, they found two notes written in an encrypted code.

The encoded messages remain unbroken despite the best efforts of FBI analysts and the American Cryptogram Association. It's possible they contain information about who killed McCormick or whether he was meeting someone the night of his murder.

In 2011, the FBI released copies of the notes to see if the general public or hobbyist codebreakers might have some insights. Applying the usual techniques to the cipher had failed to yield any usable data. Like many other encrypted messages, there wasn't enough source material to properly understand the basis of the code.

The two pages found on McCormick's body include letters, numbers, and parentheses. All characters were originally produced by hand. This is perplexing since McCormick's relatives insisted he only knew how to write his name.

In the end, the notes could be gibberish with no underlying message at all. However, the deliberate way they're organized suggests some deeper meaning. Some characters also appear to be corrected, as though McCormick originally wrote an incorrect letter and fixed it.

[47]
THE BEALE CIPHERS: TREASURE OR TALL TALE?

The story of the Beale ciphers claims that a group of Virginians were hunting near New Mexico and Colorado when they discovered gold and silver in the mountains. They extracted the precious metals and loaded them onto wagons to bring home to present-day Montvale, Virginia. One set of wagons returned in 1819, and the other followed two years later. In total, the haul is now estimated to be worth $65 million.

The group's leader, Thomas J. Beale, created three ciphers containing the location of the treasure, a description of the contents, and the recipients. Each cipher held a different piece of information. Beale entrusted the ciphers to an innkeeper before turning to the West to hunt. He promised to send along the key to decode the ciphers, but the innkeeper never received it.

After decades passed without any sign of Beale, the innkeeper turned them over to a friend who was able to solve the second cipher. It revealed what the cache entailed. He wasted a substantial amount of money attempting to break the remaining two but was unsuccessful.

Eventually, a man named James B. Ward came to own the ciphers. He published them in 1885, sparking global interest in the lost treasure. Some believe the gold and silver are still hidden near Bedford County, while others assert it's nothing more than a hoax.

Skeptics also note that the style and tone of the cipher is suspiciously close to Ward's. This could mean Ward invented the entire tale for his own financial gain. He charged money for copies of the ciphers, which could have turned a tidy profit given the initial interest in Beale's lost fortune.

[48]
THE DORABELLA CIPHER: ELGAR'S MYSTERIOUS NOTE

The composer Edward Elgar was intrigued by cryptology and the idea of hiding secret messages in unusual places. In the late 1890s, he wrote the Enigma Variations, a musical cryptogram with 14 distinct sections. Each was dedicated to one of Elgar's friends, and the composition served as the basis for naming the Enigma cipher machine used by the Nazis in World War II.

Cryptologists have unraveled most of the secrets in the Enigma Variations, but another of Elgar's puzzles remains unsolved. A letter he wrote in 1897 to a friend named Dora "Dorabella" Penny contained a cipher just for her. It's unlikely to have any major significance, but many people find it intriguing simply because of its age.

The cipher contains 24 unique symbols with a squiggle shape that vaguely resembles the letter *E*. There are 80 characters in the message spread across three rows. Elgar recorded the key in his notes, but when it's applied to the actual cipher, it results in gibberish.

One theory is that the cipher itself produces a message in a language Elgar thought only Dorabella would be able to understand. That would make it impossible for anyone else to read their letters, even if they cracked the cipher. A famous cryptoanalyst who studied the cipher also believes the message includes slang and references to inside jokes.

Since the message is relatively short, cryptologists doubt it will ever be deciphered since it lacks enough data to analyze. In fact, even Dorabella herself was unable to discern the meaning behind the cipher.

CHAPTER SIX:
HAUNTING HISTORIES

[49]
THE GHOSTS OF THE TOWER OF LONDON: ANNE BOLEYN AND MORE

William the Conqueror built the Tower of London as a symbol of his power and authority in the 1070s. Although it's most famous as a prison, the tower has also served as a palace and a place to store precious possessions. It's said there are 13 ghosts in the Tower of London, but not all of them are as well-known as Sir Walter Raleigh. In fact, some of them aren't even human.

Anne Boleyn is one of the most notable people to have been seen on the premises. She was beheaded by the infamous Henry VIII after being accused of adultery. In the late nineteenth century, a soldier went to the chapel to investigate after seeing a light inside. When he looked through the window, he saw the headless figure of Anne Boleyn leading an otherworldly procession through the church.

Anne Boleyn isn't the only ghostly ruler within the Tower of London. Lady Jane Grey, who was queen for only nine days, was executed with her husband outside the tower in 1554. Henry VI was murdered during his imprisonment in the tower. These monarchs join the uncrowned king, Edward V, and his brother, the Duke of York, who were sent to the tower and never seen again.

Even a bear is rumored to appear in the Tower of London. Henry III used the tower to house his collection of exotic animals, including lions, jackals, an elephant, and bears. Bear baiting was seen as a sport during the sixteenth and seventeenth centuries. The ghost of a bear haunts the Jewel House, where the Crown Jewels are kept.

[50]
THE *MARY CELESTE*:
THEORIES ON THE DISAPPEARING CREW

On November 7, 1872, the American brigantine *Mary Celeste* departed New York with seven sailors under the command of Captain Benjamin Spooner Briggs. His wife and their two-year-old daughter were also on board.

In early December, a British ship named the *Dei Gratia* was sailing east of the Azores archipelago when it happened upon the *Mary Celeste*. The captain of the *Dei Gratia* worried that something might have gone wrong for the ship to be so delayed and sent a crew over to offer their assistance.

When the sailors arrived, they found the *Mary Celeste* nearly untouched. The crew's personal possessions and the ship's cargo were still on board, but there was no one to be found. The lone lifeboat was missing, suggesting the men may have abandoned the ship. The reason was unclear since there was more than enough food and fresh water aboard to make it to their destination.

The last log had been made on November 24, indicating the ship had been adrift for ten full days. All other paperwork was missing. The *Dei Gratia* brought the *Mary Celeste* to Gibraltar, a journey of approximately 800 miles.

If there were any survivors from the *Mary Celeste*, none are known at this time. Some historians believe the crew became overwhelmed by vapor from the barrels of industrial alcohol they were carrying as cargo. If they were concerned that the vapor might cause an explosion on board, they might have evacuated to the lifeboat and somehow become separated from the main ship.

Although the *Mary Celeste* was fit to sail again in 1873, many viewed it as a ghost ship with a curse. Its crew intentionally wrecked it in 1885 to claim the insurance money, but the "accident" was determined to be a fraud.

[51]
THE AMITYVILLE HAUNTING: SORTING FACTS FROM FICTION

On November 13, 1974, there was a gruesome mass murder in Amityville, a suburb of New York City. Ronald Joseph DeFeo Jr. shot his four siblings and his parents before running to a nearby bar and claiming a mob hitman had broken in. Since his great-uncle was affiliated with organized crime, it was a potentially credible story.

However, the man DeFeo accused had a solid alibi. When police confronted him about his version of events, he confessed to killing his family and concealing the evidence. He was subsequently convicted to 25 years to life in prison.

Kathy and George Lutz bought the house on Ocean Avenue a little over a year later. They only lived in the home for 28 days before leaving due to paranormal activity. The Lutz family claimed there were cold spots and reported seeing a creature with red eyes that resembled a pig.

Their lawyer later alleged he, Kathy, and George made up the stories. Since the Lutzes had financial issues, it's possible they invented rumors of paranormal activity to inflate the value of their property. Notably, they both took polygraph tests and passed.

However, the next owners of the house, the Cromartys, insisted it was an ordinary home without any strange phenomena. When Jay Anson published *The Amityville Horror* in 1977, with a blockbuster film to follow two years later, the Cromartys sued the Lutzes, the author, and the publishing company for making false claims. The lawsuit was settled out of court.

Even if the home in Amityville isn't subject to supernatural forces, its reputation as one of the most haunted places in the country persists. The Cromartys were so inundated with tourists and fans that they even changed the address to better protect their privacy.

[52]
THE BELL WITCH:
A POLTERGEIST IN TENNESSEE

In 1804, a farmer named John Bell moved to Adams, TN, with his family. They had a quiet life until 1817, when they started to notice paranormal activity around their farm. The Bells heard chains dragging across the floor and saw unusual creatures at night. At last, they traced the mysterious events to a witch known only as Kate.

Kate specifically tormented John and his daughter, Betsy. Researchers believe Kate wanted to kill John and prevent Betsy from marrying the neighbor, but no motive has been uncovered for either. Nonetheless, John Bell died in 1820, and Betsy decided not to marry the neighbor after her father's death.

According to a written account by John Bell's son, Kate left behind poison and acknowledged that she had killed John. The family fed the poison to a cat to see if her claims were true, and the cat died as well. With John dead and Betsy's engagement called off, Kate gradually disappeared and stopped haunting the Bells.

Betsy passed down some of her stories to her great-nephew Charles Bailey Bell. He wrote a book about how Kate visited the family again in 1828 to pass along prophecies for the future. Kate said she would return in 1935.

Interestingly, the year 1935 passed without any notable sightings of the Bell Witch. Instead, there were multiple incidents reported two years later. A local group was having an event near the site of the Bell property when they saw Kate standing on the rocks above them. The owner of the Bell farm also reported hearing strange noises from the cave on his property. Some people believe Kate is still within the town of Adams, destined to return again.

[53]
THE CHASE FAMILY CRYPT: COFFINS THAT WOULDN'T STAY PUT

Located in Oistins, Barbados, the Chase family crypt is said to hold coffins that move of their own accord. The family purchased the vault in 1724 when two-year-old Mary Ann Chase died. There was one other coffin already inside when it was sold. Within a few years, Mary Ann's sister starved herself to death and was interred in the crypt as well.

A month later, Mary Ann's father passed away as well. When workers opened the crypt, they were stunned to discover that the three coffins were upright against the wall. They couldn't find any evidence that someone had broken into the vault, and none of the other graves nearby had been disturbed.

It seemed unlikely that an earthquake or another natural cause had moved the coffins in only one area. It was far more probable for vandals to have broken in, but there weren't any valuables stored inside for them to steal.

The phenomenon continued for every subsequent burial. The surviving members of the Chase family tried everything they could to solve the mystery. They put down sand that would show footprints and checked the crypt for secret entrances. The governor of Barbados even placed his seal on the vault in 1819 after a burial to prove the opening remained undisturbed.

But when the Chases experienced another death, the coffins were still in new locations with no sign of entry. Eventually, the family removed the remains of their loved ones and buried them elsewhere. The vault remains empty, and the late Chase family members have remained undisturbed in their new resting places.

[54]
THE BROWN LADY OF RAYNHAM HALL:
THE FAMOUS GHOST PHOTOGRAPH

The day after Christmas in 1936, *Country Life* magazine shocked the world when it published a photograph of the ghost known as the Brown Lady of Raynham Hall. Rumors that the mansion in Norfolk, England, was haunted stretched back into the 1800s, but capturing proof wasn't the original intent of the photographers.

In fact, Captain Hubert Provand and his assistant Indre Shira had simply been working on a general interest piece about Raynham Hall when they spotted the apparition in a photograph of the staircase. Locals familiar with the haunting of Raynham Hall already knew it to be Lady Lady Townshend, the wife of a viscount who allegedly locked her away for the remainder of her life after discovering her adultery.

She'd earned the name "the Brown Lady" after several witnesses reported seeing a ghost walking Raynham Hall in a brown dress. In 1835, multiple guests at a Christmas party saw the spirit of Lady Townshend as they were heading to their rooms to sleep.

A year later, naval captain Frederick Marryat insisted on proving that the ghost was really the work of smugglers trying to scare any visitors away from Norfolk. Not only did Captain Marryat fail, but he ended up attempting to shoot the Brown Lady after seeing her in the hallway.

But ever since her image was published in *Country Life* in 1936, Lady Townshend rarely appeared again at Raynham Hall. Instead, many people now speculate that the ghost has moved on to nearby country homes, where she appears as a younger version of her former self.

[55]
BORLEY RECTORY: THE MOST HAUNTED HOUSE IN ENGLAND

In 1863, Reverend Henry Bull built Borley Rectory on the site of a former monastery in the town of Borley, Essex. Rumors say a nun who lived in a nearby convent fell in love with a monk from the old monastery. The two attempted to elope, but they were caught and sentenced to death. The monk was hanged, and the nun was sealed away alive within the walls of the nunnery.

Four of the reverend's daughters were out one night in the summer of 1900 when they saw the nun wandering the grounds. The apparition vanished when they attempted to speak with her. The organist for the church also remarked that others in the Bull family had seen the ghost multiple times. Local residents even reported seeing headless horsemen driving a coach in the area around the rectory.

After the Bulls, the Reverend Guy Eric Smith and his wife were the next people to inhabit Borley Rectory. Smith contacted the newspaper in 1928 to chronicle the strange phenomena he'd noticed throughout the house. The *Daily Mirror* hired the psychic expert Harry Price to investigate the situation. Price called it "the most haunted house in England."

The Smiths soon departed and were replaced in late 1930 by the family of Reverend Lionel Algernon Foyster, a relative of the Bulls. The Foysters were struck by stones and attacked by some unseen force. The situation became so desperate that the reverend attempted exorcisms on two occasions.

The house was finally destroyed by a fire in 1939, much like the fire that had burned down the previous rectory in 1841. The Borley Rectory remained abandoned until 1944, when it was eventually torn down.

[56]
THE MYRTLES PLANTATION: A HAUNTED HISTORY

Clarke Woodruff and his wife moved to the Laural Grove plantation in St. Francisville, Louisiana, in 1817. Stories claim they owned a slave named Chloe, whom they treated cruelly and abused. When Chloe was caught eavesdropping on their conversations, Woodruff cut off one of her ears. Chloe wore a green turban after that to conceal the wound.

During a birthday party, Chloe baked a cake with oleander leaves, resulting in the death of Woodruff's wife and two of their children. To avoid being accused of collusion, the other slaves captured Chloe and hanged her. They threw her body into the river. Ever since, visitors to the renamed Myrtles Plantation have reported seeing the ghost of Chloe.

Other versions of the story claim that Myrtles Plantation was actually built on an Indigenous burial ground belonging to the Tunica peoples who lived in the region. That version of the tale refers to the fact that Sara Woodruff and her children died of yellow fever, according to historical records.

The gruesome legacy of the plantation continued even after the Woodruffs sold it. During the Civil War, the new owners hired an attorney named William Winter to review the financial accounts of the plantation.

In 1871, a man rode up to the porch where the attorney was standing and fatally shot him with no known motive. Winter crawled inside for help before dying on the staircase. His spirit is only one of many haunting the grounds and halls of the Myrtles Plantation.

[57]
THE TALE OF LA LLORONA:
A WEEPING SPIRIT

The tale of La Llorona tells the story of a beautiful woman named Maria. Many men were eager to call her their own, but she eventually married and had two sons. But after their family grew, Maria's husband became disinterested in her and only paid attention to the boys.

Some versions say that he was having an affair with a woman of status, while another states he simply wanted to live like he was single again. Maria became so angry that she threw her children into the river. She may have wanted to kill them, or she might have underestimated the strength of the current. Both her sons were carried away by the water.

The legend says that Maria wandered the banks of the river, waiting for them to return. She refused to leave, even to eat or sleep, until her eventual death. It's said the spirit of La Llorona wanders from river to lake in search of her drowned children.

Many people have claimed to see a crying woman in a white dress by the water. Despite her grief, she's far from harmless. Parents warn their children that La Llorana will drag them into the water if they get too close.

In Santa Fe, New Mexico, La Llorona is notorious for appearing on land built near an old cemetery along the river. Several employees have reported hearing her crying in the hallways and stairwells. Sightings of Maria's spirit range as far away as the Yellowstone River.

[58]
THE HAUNTINGS OF THE STANLEY HOTEL:
INSPIRATION FOR *THE SHINING*

At the turn of the twentieth century, entrepreneur Freelan Oscar Stanley was searching for a way to alleviate the symptoms of his tuberculosis. Since doctors often recommended fresh air and sunlight, Stanley and his wife traveled to Colorado. After his health significantly improved, he decided to create a resort in the mountains where guests could relax or recuperate.

The Stanley Hotel opened in 1909 in the town of Estes Park. Two years later, the gas lighting system caused an explosion, and a maid named Elizabeth Wilson fell from room 217 to the floor below. Although Wilson survived the encounter, guests have reported seeing her ghost in room 217 and experiencing strange phenomena like the lights turning off or items moving without explanation.

The fourth floor of the hotel was originally quite popular with nannies and the children they cared for. In the present day, some guests still hear laughter or the sound of children running back and forth. Rooms 401, 407, and 428 are so haunted that the hotel allows guests to specifically request them while making a reservation.

It's even said that the ghosts of Freelan Oscar Stanley and his wife Flora are still on the premises. Freelan is sometimes seen at the check-in desk, while Flora has been known to play the piano. Flora passed away in 1939, and Freelan followed a year later.

Given such a colorful history of paranormal happenings, it's unsurprising that the Stanley Hotel served as the inspiration for Stephen King's *The Shining*. While staying in room 217, King had a nightmare about a fire hose chasing his son through the hallways. The movie starring Jack Nicholson was filmed elsewhere, but King later created his own miniseries shot at the Stanley Hotel.

CHAPTER SEVEN: HISTORICAL ENIGMAS

[59]
STONEHENGE: CONSTRUCTION AND ALIGNMENT THEORIES

Stonehenge was built in modern-day Salisbury Plain in southern England over the course of hundreds of years, roughly between 3000 BCE and 1520 BCE. Its construction took place in both the Neolithic Period and the Bronze Age.

The monument features two distinct rings. The outer circle is made of upright sarsen stones topped by horizontal ones. The inner ring is made of much shorter, smaller bluestones. Only 52 sarsen stones remain, but there might have been over 80 when Stonehenge was first constructed.

The first archaeological investigation took place in the 1660s when John Aubrey analyzed the origins of the stones. He incorrectly believed Stonehenge had been built by Celts and Druid priests. Modern dating techniques, however, proved that Stonehenge was assembled approximately 1,000 years before Celts settled in the area.

Some of the sarsen stones weigh up to four tons. Since humans hadn't yet invented the wheel, historians have long wondered how they transported such large stones over great distances. In 2010, an engineer proposed that Neolithic builders used wicker slings and baskets to move stones into configuration.

The meaning of how the stones are aligned is also a mystery. The sarsen stones are known to manipulate and produce sound, suggesting music or long-distance communication could play a role. Since Stonehenge faces toward the rising sun during the summer solstice, another theory is that the stones make up a form of calendar.

Mike Parker Pearson, one of the leaders of the Stonehenge Riverside Project, believes Stonehenge was half of a pair. The circles match a wooden circle at Durrington Walls that would have been connected to Stonehenge by the River Avon. Pearson suggests the two monuments are meant to represent life and death.

[60]
THE SHROUD OF TURIN: SCIENTIFIC INVESTIGATIONS AND DEBATES

The Shroud of Turin is one of Christianity's most important relics, but it didn't appear in any historical records until the 1350s. A French knight brought the shroud to Lirey, France, and gave it to the church's dean, describing it as the burial shroud of Jesus. The cloth features the outline of Jesus's body after the crucifixion. Believers claim the body of Christ radiated light and caused the image to imprint on the shroud.

Although Pope Clement VII declared it wasn't authentic in 1389, many people still argue that the evidence isn't conclusive. In the 1970s, researchers noted that the markings match the wounds from crucifixion, and the stains on the shroud are human blood. The Vatican continues to refer to the shroud as a religious icon rather than a relic.

Estimates of the fabric's age are inconsistent. One organization claims the shroud was made between 1260 and 1390, while another group believes it could date back as far as 300 BCE. Since the shroud was repaired in medieval times after a fire, it's possible that samples could provide conflicting results.

In 2018, a forensic anthropologist and a chemist attempted to recreate the bloodstains on the fabric. They were unable to replicate the markings from the shroud, causing them to doubt whether the bloodstains were really made by wrapping a body. Other experts have challenged the study, noting that no one knows exactly how Jesus's body was handled, moved, or covered.

In the future, more advanced analytical technologies may yield new information to settle the dispute about the true origins of the Shroud of Turin. Until then, it remains a historically significant artifact of great religious importance regardless of its authenticity.

[61]
THE TERRACOTTA ARMY: CREATION AND UNKNOWN CHAMBERS

The first emperor of China, Qin Shi Huang, was obsessed with the idea of eternal life and finding a source of immortality. At the same time, he was dedicated to creating a massive tomb for himself that spanned 3.9 square miles. The emperor died in the year 210 BCE.

The underground complex was discovered accidentally in 1974 by farmers attempting to dig a well. The pits are filled with more than 8,000 soldiers made of terracotta, and each one is unique in some way. Their heights, ages, and facial features all vary widely. In addition to soldiers, there are also terracotta administrators, acrobats, and animal attendants.

The tomb complex even includes a stable with the remains of hundreds of horses that were sacrificed. Attendants made of ceramic populate the stable, and archaeologists have found the remnants of hay inside as well. Other nearby pits contain the remains of birds, deer, and exotic species that most likely came from the emperor's zoo.

Additionally, there are smaller tombs that historians believe belong to the emperor's relatives or concubines. Hundreds of workers and prisoners were also entombed in the area. Some are labeled by rank or criminal sentence depending on the person's status.

Even after decades of excavating the mausoleum, some areas have never been opened or explored. Historians have left the emperor's burial chamber sealed because they're concerned about being able to properly preserve and protect its contents. Advanced methods like magnetic anomaly surveying have yielded basic information about the layout and size of the chamber.

[62]
PRINCES IN THE TOWER: DISAPPEARANCES AND DEATHS

King Edward IV of England died on April 9, 1483. He temporarily entrusted the throne to his brother, Richard, to serve as regent until his son, Edward V, came of age. On May 10, Edward V arrived at the Tower of London to prepare for his upcoming coronation.

Richard began promoting his supporters to strategic positions of power. When key leaders refused to support Richard's claim to the throne, he had them arrested or executed. He also brought Edward V's younger brother, Richard of Shrewsbury, to the Tower of London under the guise of preparing for the coronation.

A bishop came forward on June 8 to point out that the late King Edward IV had agreed to marry someone else before his wedding to Elizabeth Woodville, rendering any children from their union illegitimate. The children of Edward IV's next brother in the line of succession were deemed ineligible as well because of crimes committed by their father, the Duke of Clarence.

Parliament eventually accepted Richard's case that he was the true heir and named him the rightful king on June 25. The two young princes were never seen in public again. Most historians assume the king had them killed to avoid any challenges for the throne.

However, the king of Portugal's secretary claimed the boys starved to death after being turned over to Henry Stafford, an early supporter of King Richard III, who later sought to overthrow him. Because of this change in allegiances, it's unclear whether he would have helped or hurt the young princes.

There are two sets of remains that could belong to the princes. King Charles III has indicated he's receptive to the idea of conducting testing to determine whether the remains belong to Edward V and his brother Richard of Shrewsbury.

[63]
THE DANCING PLAGUE OF 1518: ORIGINS AND THEORIES

In the summer of 1518, a woman named Frau Troffea started dancing in the public square in the French town of Strasbourg. She supposedly danced for almost a full week, barely noticing fatigue or pain. Within a month, hundreds of other people joined.

As the dance went on, up to 15 people per day were dying from overexertion and heart attacks. Others simply collapsed when they couldn't continue. The local authorities were baffled as they searched for solutions. They brought a group of dancers to a shrine outside the city limits and waited until they stopped dancing. Eventually, the remaining people in the square stopped as well.

Bizarrely, this wasn't the only dancing plague to affect Europe in the sixteenth and seventeenth centuries. Researchers have even questioned whether toxins in food could have caused people to hallucinate or become especially animated. Others believe the 1518 dancing plague was a form of mass hysteria due to harsh living conditions, poor crop yields, and other stressors.

There is some potential for the idea of stress causing mass psychogenic illness. In 1962, up to 1,000 people were affected by the Tanganyika laughter epidemic. The country had just won its short-lived independence, and many people were struggling to adapt.

The true cause of the dancing plague remains unknown, but the power of the mind and social pressure shouldn't be underestimated. According to psychologists, mass hysteria is especially likely to occur when disadvantaged groups have no other means of expression or control over their circumstances.

[64]
THE OSEBERG SHIP BURIAL: A VIKING ENIGMA

In August 1903, a farmer named Knut Rom was digging on his property when he found a unique wooden fragment with unusual carvings. He traveled to Oslo with the piece of wood to consult a professor at the University Museum of National Antiquities. The professor was so shocked by the carvings on the wood that he went to Rom's farm the next day to validate the discovery of a Viking ship burial.

The ship had originally been buried using clay, which trapped enough moisture to preserve the wood and many of the artifacts inside. The ship itself measured 70 feet in length and 16 feet in width. After analysis, researchers learned that the wood dated back to 834 C.E.

Unfortunately, grave robbers had already broken into the ship, most likely in a time contemporary with the original burial ceremony. Most of the valuables were missing, but since textiles break down easily over time, the fabrics onboard were extremely valuable from a historical perspective. Besides textiles, the ship also contained a cart, the remains of livestock, farming tools, tents, and other everyday items the dead might require in the afterlife.

Archaeologists found the bodies of two women on the ship, but their identities are a mystery. Many historians believe the ship to be the grave of Queen Åsa, the grandmother of Norway's first king. Others suggest it was in honor of a high priestess.

Regardless, it's obvious from the finery and riches that at least one of the women was held in high esteem in Viking society. Even if their identities are never uncovered, the ship was an important cultural find that provides a glimpse into the life of the first century.

[65]
THE VINLAND MAP:
AUTHENTIC OR FORGERY?

The first mentions of the Vinland map were in 1957 when it appeared alongside a smaller volume called the *Tartar Relation*. Book dealer Irving Davis offered it to the British Museum, but the museum was skeptical of its authenticity because the bindings and markings weren't consistent. It declined to buy the map, resulting in its sale to another book dealer named Laurence Witten II.

Witten had graduated from Yale University, so he approached Thomas Marston, a curator at the school's library. Marston shared the same concerns expressed by the museum until he realized a volume purchased from Davis must have been part of a set with the Vinland map and the *Tartar Relation*. When all three items were put together, the markings appeared to match.

The authenticity of the Vinland map was incredibly important because it was the earliest known map to depict the Americas. That information had the potential to change the modern perception of history. Marston and two other experts who authored a book on the map estimated that it was made in approximately the year 1440 CE.

However, historians were divided about the origins and authenticity of the map, so the Smithsonian Institute held a conference in 1966 to hear arguments from either side. The matter wasn't definitively settled until 2021, when new analytical techniques revealed the ink on the Vinland map uses a compound that wasn't in use until the 1920s.

The analysis of the map also showed that historical inscriptions were modified to make the map appear as old as the book it was bound with. The paper itself was authentic, suggesting the unknown forger took advantage of the aged paper to create a convincing fake.

[66]
THE SEA PEOPLES:
THE UNKNOWN INVADERS OF ANCIENT CIVILIZATIONS

The Sea Peoples were a group of raiders who targeted Egypt and the greater Mediterranean region. Historians have long wondered about the period ranging from the late Bronze Age to the start of the Iron Age and what might have caused the widespread collapse of civilizations like the Hittite Empire and the Amorite states. Drought and natural disasters may have played a role, but the Sea Peoples are also potential culprits.

These raiders were active from 1276 BCE to 1178 BCE, and they were especially interested in Egypt. Egyptian records confirm the existence of the Sea Peoples on multiple occasions, but they don't expand upon their origins. The Sea Peoples could have come from Southern Europe, Anatolia, the Aegean, or the islands throughout the Mediterranean.

The Sea Peoples may also have worked as mercenaries. In 1274 BCE, Ramesses the Great (Ramesses II) went to war with the Hittites over the city of Kadesh in modern-day Syria. Kadesh was an important trade hub in the ancient world. Historical accounts of the conflict mention the Sea Peoples, stating that they fought with Ramesses the Great as mercenaries but also appeared on the side of the Hittites.

This suggests world leaders were willing to ally themselves with the Sea Peoples because of their prowess on the battlefield, even if the Sea Peoples had been their enemies in the past. It also reinforces the idea that the Sea Peoples had no permanent allegiances to a particular ruler or kingdom.

In 1178 BCE, Ramesses III defeated the Sea Peoples in a battle at Xois during their invasion of Egypt. However, the war was so expensive that Ramesses III was unable to pay wages to the teams of tomb builders who lived in the village of Set Maat. They refused to continue working until they were paid in the first known labor strike in history.

[67]
CLEOPATRA'S LOST TOMB: AN ANCIENT MYSTERY

Cleopatra is one of the most famous figures from ancient Egypt for good reason. By the age of 18, she had already become queen and learned to speak up to a dozen languages. By 21, she was leading an army and maneuvering against her younger brother in a civil war to reclaim the Egyptian throne.

She allied with Julius Caesar, and the two had a son, Ptolemy Caesar, who was better known by the nickname "Caesarion." After Caesar's murder, three of his supporters—Mark Antony, Octavian, and Lepidus—sought to keep power away from those who had conspired against him.

Cleopatra and Mark Antony became lovers and entered a politically advantageous relationship. Cleopatra sent troops to fight for Caesar's surviving allies, while Antony promised to keep her in power in Egypt. When Antony backed Caesarion as Caesar's true heir, he all but declared war on Octavian, Caesar's adopted son and the future Emperor Augustus I.

After almost a year of fighting, Octavian defeated Antony and Cleopatra in 31 BCE. Antony committed suicide after hearing a false rumor that Cleopatra had already killed herself. Cleopatra buried him in an unknown location and took her own life at the age of 39, reportedly by using a venomous snake. She was entombed alongside Antony, and the site of their final resting place has never been found.

However, in November 2022, a team of archaeologists discovered a tunnel by the Taposiris Magna temple that could eventually lead to Cleopatra's tomb. Archaeologist Kathleen Martínez believes the tomb may be underwater after damage to the coastlines caused parts of the Taposiris Magna complex to sink.

[68]
THE ARK OF THE COVENANT: UNCERTAIN FATE

The Ark of the Covenant is an acacia chest covered in pure gold that was created by the Israelites to store the stone tablets bearing the Ten Commandments. The Ark has two angels on top and attached rings to carry it with poles.

The Ark has been connected to multiple miracles that took place in the Old Testament. The Israelites carried it as they journeyed to the Promised Land in Exodus, and the Ark cleared obstacles and dangers along their path. The chest was later stored at the Temple of Jerusalem until the Babylonians attacked and sacked the temple in approximately 586 BCE.

The Israelites moved the Ark around that time, but its whereabouts have been lost to history. There are multiple theories in the modern day about its possible location. St. Mary of Zion church in Aksum, Ethiopia, claims to have the Ark of the Covenant but attests that only its guardian is permitted to view it. The church has never agreed to testing or authentication.

Another theory is that the Ark is hidden in underground passageways in Jerusalem that run underneath the First Temple. However, since the Dome of the Rock is located on top, there's no way to access the underground areas, especially since the dome is sacred in Islam.

Some historians also believe the Ark may have fallen into the hands of the Babylonians. According to the *Greek Apocalypse of Ezra*, the army took any precious metals and valuables they found in the Temple of Jerusalem. That could mean the Ark of the Covenant eventually made its way to modern-day Baghdad.

CHAPTER EIGHT: POLITICAL PUZZLES

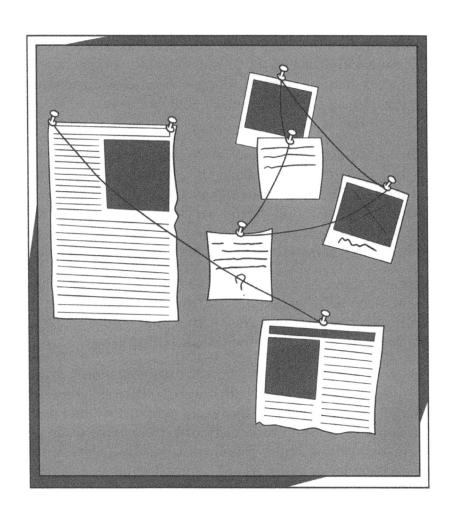

[69]
THE JFK ASSASSINATION: THE GRASSY KNOLL AND THE MAGIC BULLET THEORY

President John F. Kennedy Jr. was assassinated on November 22, 1963, while riding in a motorcade in Dallas. Lee Harvey Oswald was charged with firing on the president by the Texas School Book Depository, where he worked filling orders. Oswald insisted he was being framed, but he was fatally shot two days later before he could stand trial.

Despite the official story, many witnesses claimed to have seen smoke or heard gunshots in the vicinity of the grassy knoll ahead of the motorcade. This led to theories that there was a second shooter. In 2023, a former Secret Service agent who was riding behind the presidential car admitted to having doubts about whether Oswald was the only gunman involved.

He claimed to have moved a bullet from the back of the president's seat that eventually ended up on the stretcher holding John Connally, the governor of Texas. If true, that would weaken the official version of events and the "magic bullet theory."

The government investigation into the assassination concluded that Oswald fired three shots, with only two striking the president. One bullet hit Kennedy in the head, while the other hit the president in the back and continued forward to injure Connally in the front seat. If the bullet found on Connally's stretcher only ended up there accidentally, it could suggest someone else shot the governor.

During interviews, Connally himself opposed the single-bullet theory despite agreeing that Oswald acted alone. The Select

Committee on Assassinations, however, noted that acoustic analysis returned a high probability of multiple shooters firing on the motorcade.

[70]
THE FATE OF THE AMBER ROOM: THEORIES OF ITS CURRENT LOCATION

During World War II, the Nazis looted and stole over half a million works of art. A set of priceless panels collectively known as the Amber Room remains missing to this day. The panels originally adorned the walls of the Catherine Palace in Tsarskoye Selo, Russia.

As the Nazis advanced into Russia, the palace's head curator was instructed to carefully disassemble the Amber Room and prepare it for transport to a safer region. He soon realized the panels were too fragile to remove. Instead, the Russians covered the amber with wallpaper and hoped none of the Nazis would know of the Amber Room's existence.

However, the Nazis knew to search for the panels since they were originally created in the early 1700s. The Nazis were able to successfully remove and pack the panels. They sent the Amber Room to Königsberg, the German city that later became Kaliningrad, Russia, in the post-war years. The amber panels were put on display in the castle until Hitler ordered all items of value to be removed from Königsberg.

The war was turning in favor of the Allies, and the Royal Air Force bombed Königsberg in 1944. The castle was also damaged by Soviet artillery in 1945. When Russian forces reached the castle, the Amber Room was gone, but it's possible the panels were simply destroyed.

Alexander Brusov, a professor who was sent to retrieve looted art from the castle, found multiple burned mosaics that once belonged to the Amber Room. This suggests the panels were too badly damaged to save.

Some people claimed to have witnessed the panels being loaded onto a ship called the *Wilhelm Gustloff* that was sunk by a Soviet submarine off the coast of Poland. Divers have investigated the wreck but failed to find any sign of amber.

[71]
JIMMY HOFFA'S LAST DAYS: LEADS, SPECULATIONS, AND FALSE CLAIMS

Jimmy Hoffa was a famous union leader with ties to organized crime. After taking a job at a Kroger grocery warehouse at the age of 14, he rose through the ranks to become the president of the International Brotherhood of Teamsters before he even turned 30 years old.

In 1967, Hoffa was sentenced to 13 years in prison on charges of fraud and conspiracy, among others. President Nixon commuted his sentence in December 1971 on the condition that Hoffa wouldn't pursue union leadership until the time when his prison term would have ended.

Hoffa swore he never agreed to forego union activities and immediately attempted to leverage his connections with organized crime to regain his former position. On July 30, 1975, he scheduled a meeting with the New Jersey–based Provenzano family and the Giacolones from Detroit.

He called his wife while waiting at the Machus Red Fox restaurant in Bloomfield, Michigan, and multiple people claimed to have seen him in the parking lot. One witness watched Hoffa get into a vehicle with three unidentified passengers. Hoffa didn't return home that night, prompting the police to declare him officially missing on July 31. His body was never found.

Authorities suspected that Chuckie O'Brien, a friend who had broken ties with Hoffa, participated in his murder. However, former US Assistant Attorney General Jack Goldsmith believes Vito Giacalone, the brother of Detroit mafia leader Anthony Giacalone, was truly responsible.

Goldsmith's theory is especially interesting since he's the stepson of Chuckie O'Brien, making him far from an impartial voice despite his professional accolades as an accomplished attorney and Harvard professor. Goldsmith claims the FBI eventually determined O'Brien wasn't guilty but wanted to avoid the backlash of making a faulty accusation in such a high-profile case.

[72]
NAPOLEON BONAPARTE: THE NOTORIOUS LEADER'S CAUSE OF DEATH

Napoleon Bonaparte rose to power during the French Revolution and served as the Emperor of the French from 1804 to 1814 and again for a short period in 1815. He was defeated at Waterloo in 1815 and banished to Saint Helena, an extremely remote island to the west of Africa in the South Atlantic Ocean.

Since Napoleon had already escaped once while exiled to Elba, security measures were especially strict. He lived in a rundown mansion that was damp and drafty. The island itself also had an infestation of rats.

After living there for roughly five and a half years, Napoleon was acutely aware of his declining health. He even reconnected with the Catholic Church to prepare for his last rites ahead of his death on May 5, 1821, at the age of 51.

Napoleon's doctor, Francesco Antommarchi, conducted an autopsy and listed the cause of death as stomach cancer. An alternate theory emerged in the 1960s when a Swedish toxicologist named Sten Forshufvud theorized that Napoleon might actually have been killed by arsenic poisoning.

Strands of Napoleon's hair collected in 1805 and 1820 showed high levels of arsenic. Since no one else on Saint Helena exhibited symptoms of arsenic poisoning, Forshufvud's research suggested that Napoleon was specifically targeted.

A professor concurred in 1994, pointing out that Napoleon was the only person on the island who drank a particular type of wine. That would have made it simple to poison him without harming any others in the house.

However, many historians remain doubtful about these assertions due to the high levels of arsenic in household products during the nineteenth century. With few regulations on food, drugs, or cosmetics, it's possible that Napoleon's chronic overexposure to arsenic resulted from his own habits.

[73]
MARTIN BORMANN'S DISAPPEARANCE: ESCAPE, SIGHTINGS, AND DNA

Martin Bormann was Hitler's personal secretary, making him one of the Nazi dictator's closest staff members. After Hitler took his own life in April 1945, Bormann attempted to flee Berlin along with Hitler Youth leader Artur Axmann and the SS doctor Ludwig Stumpfegger.

Axmann became separated upon reaching Lehrter Station. When he ran to a nearby bridge, he saw two bodies that he assumed were the corpses of Bormann and Stumpfegger, but he didn't delay looking at them closely since he was fleeing the Soviets.

However, the Soviet Union never confirmed finding Bormann's body. Multiple people claimed to have seen him in Europe and South America over the following decades. The matter was almost settled in 1972 when construction workers found two bodies close to where Axmann had reported seeing Bormann.

Dental records confirmed it was Bormann, and the other skeleton fit Stumpfegger's general height and physical size. Examiners also found glass that suggested they'd died after taking cyanide pills.

However, an author named Hugh Thomas cast doubt on that story in 1995 when he questioned why Bormann's skull had been covered in a red clay native to Paraguay. Thomas also asserted that the dental analyses of Bormann's body showed dental work that was far more recent than 1945. Other historians believe that Bormann lived in South America for several years before his body was smuggled back to Berlin.

In 1998, the German government conducted DNA testing by comparing samples from Bormann's body to one of his relatives. The results definitively established that the body belonged to Bormann. However, whether or not he truly died in 1945 remains a mystery.

[74]
GRAND DUCHESS ANASTASIA: DID SHE ESCAPE THE BOLSHEVIKS?

Grand Duchess Anastasia Romanov was the fourth daughter of Nicholas II, the last tsar of Russia, and Tsarina Alexandra Feodorovna. She was born in 1901, in the final years of the Romanov dynasty. Her younger brother, Alexei, was heir.

Nicholas II rose to power in a country that was already divided. Tensions worsened during World War I as millions of soldiers and civilians were killed in the conflict. In March 1917, a group of soldiers mutinied against the tsar. After some resistance, Nicholas II agreed to abdicate to avoid further bloodshed.

The family was moved several times before reaching a rundown house in Yekaterinburg. In the summer of 1918, the family received word that they'd be relocating again. They packed their valuables in case they found an opportunity to flee. In reality, the Bolsheviks led them into the basement and killed the entire family.

Rumors began to spread that Alexei and Anastasia had survived the ordeal because the gems sewn into their clothes protected them. Multiple people came forward in the following years claiming to be Anastasia, but they lacked sufficient proof to convince the courts.

During the 1970s, an archaeologist discovered a grave with the remains of three children and half a dozen adults. He kept the grave a secret until the Soviet Union was on the verge of collapse. In 1991, investigators identified the bodies as the Romanov family and their servants. Anastasia and Alexei were missing, fueling further speculation that they'd managed to escape.

In 2007, another grave was located a short distance from the first. The grave contained the bodies of two children who were later identified as the grand duchess and her brother. It's unclear why they were buried separately, but there's no longer any doubt about the tragic fate of Anastasia.

[75]
LORD LUCAN:
CIRCUMSTANCES AND DISAPPEARANCE

Richard John Bingham, the 7th Earl of Lucan, vanished on November 8, 1974, under suspicion of murdering his children's nanny. After separating from his wife in 1972, he became increasingly unstable as he searched for a way to turn the custody ruling for their three children in his favor.

On November 7, 1974, he went to his wife's home in the Central London district of Belgravia and bludgeoned Sandra Rivett to death, most likely mistaking the nanny for his wife. He then turned on Lady Lucan. Although grievously injured in the attack, Lady Lucan was able to escape and flee the home.

Lord Lucan was last seen in East Sussex. His whereabouts after that point are unknown, but there have been numerous sightings throughout the years. Many people, including Lady Lucan, speculated that the earl might have committed suicide. In 2016, a writer named Peter James claimed to have spoken with some of Lucan's contacts and confidants.

His theory asserts that Lord Lucan's friends helped him sneak away to Switzerland. When Lord Lucan became insistent that he needed to speak with his children, his friends killed him rather than face the risk of the authorities discovering they'd aided a wanted man. Since Lord Lucan's erratic behavior started in part because of the custody battle with his wife, attempting to call his children seems consistent with his previous actions.

In 2022, Sandra Rivett's son sent pictures of Lord Lucan and an elderly Australian man to a professor at the UK's University of Bradford to see if he had potentially found Lord Lucan hiding near Brisbane. The professor used advanced facial recognition software and determined they were a match.

Officially, however, Lord Lucan is deceased. His death certificate was finally released in 2016 in order to allow his son to inherit his titles.

[76]
DAG HAMMARKJÖLD: MYSTERIOUS DEATH OF A UN SECRETARY-GENERAL

Dag Hammarskjöld was the second secretary-general of the United Nations, serving from 1953 until his untimely death less than a decade later. In the early morning hours of September 18, 1961, Hammarskjöld was traveling to the Republic of the Congo, which had just gained its independence from Belgium. The chartered plane crashed in present-day Zambia, killing Hammarskjöld and 13 other people on impact. One person survived but later succumbed to their injuries.

Although initial inquiries blamed pilot error, many speculated that Hammarskjöld was deliberately targeted. The first prime minister, Patrice Lumumba, had asked the Soviet Union for its support, pulling the Republic of the Congo into the Cold War as a proxy. The CIA and Belgium contributed to Lumumba's removal from office and subsequent assassination.

Meanwhile, a southern part of the Congo announced the intention to secede. This was worrisome since Katanga had uranium and other valuable metals. The United Nations sent forces to Katanga to oust mercenaries from the region in an action known as Operation Morthor ("Operation Murder").

The UN didn't consult several world powers in advance of the operation, causing tensions with the United States and the UK. Hammarskjöld was already in Leopoldville meeting with Lumumba's successor, so he planned a meeting with separatist leader Moise Tshombe in Katanga.

After the crash, a UN investigation couldn't rule out the possibility that Hammarskjöld's plane was shot down. The British high commissioner at Hammarskjöld's destination claimed the secretary-general had decided to change his travel plans when the plane failed to land. It's also suspicious that no ground search was launched for hours after witnesses saw signs of a crash.

President Harry Truman even said to reporters that Hammarskjöld had been killed. To date, however, there has never been definitive proof that Hammarskjöld's death wasn't an accident caused by pilot error.

CHAPTER NINE:
UNIDENTIFIED PHENOMENA

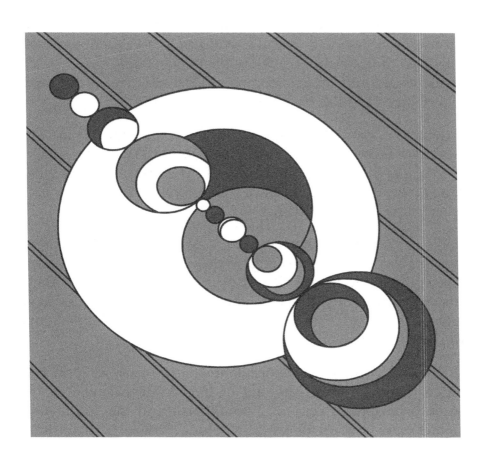

[77]
CROP CIRCLES:
HUMAN OR UNKNOWN ORIGINS

Crop circles started to appear in earnest in the 1970s and 1980s. They've been found all over the world in locations ranging from California to Indonesia. Some are relatively simple, while others are extremely intricate and complex. Most crop circles appear in fields with cereals like barley and wheat.

In the 1960s, tourists flocked to Wiltshire, the same region that encompasses Stonehenge, to look for signs of UFOs. Years later, in 1976, England inadvertently launched the crop circle craze when Doug Bower and his friend Dave Chorley created a fake nest for a flying saucer in a wheat field.

People with an active interest in crop circles are called "croppies." They search for hidden meanings in the designs, and not everyone believes the patterns are caused by human intervention. Many different theories about aliens, ghosts, and secret energies have surfaced over the years. Scientists of the late twentieth century even questioned whether radiation could play a role.

Prior to 2012, there was also speculation that crop circles contained hidden messages about the end of the Mayan calendar. Some people believed the year 2012 would usher in the apocalypse. Another view claimed the world would undergo a great spiritual transformation.

Despite the controversy about crop circles in regions like Wiltshire, they do occasionally appear from natural causes. In 2009, wallabies accidentally created crop circles in Tasmania after eating opium from a legal farm and becoming intoxicated. They hopped in circles, consuming more poppies, resulting in unusual designs.

[78]
THE TAOS HUM:
INVESTIGATIVE REPORTS AND THEORIES

In the late 1980s or early 1990s, residents in the area of Taos, New Mexico, started hearing a low hum emanating from somewhere in town. Only some people were able to detect the sound, which caused division between those who could hear the noise and those who couldn't. A group banded together and reached out to the state's congressional representatives to request an investigation.

Experts from multiple groups, including the Philips Air Force Laboratory and the University of New Mexico, went to Taos in 1993 to study the phenomenon. They interviewed people who could hear the noise and took readings from throughout the town.

Since residents used different terms to describe the noise and seemed to be referring to different types of sounds, the team couldn't draw any conclusions about the origins of the hum. In other cases where a strange sound was later identified, most witnesses had fairly consistent descriptions.

For example, people on the Pacific Island of Borneo heard noises in 2012 that sounded like roaring. They later discovered the sounds originated from a factory that was conducting maintenance testing.

One possible explanation for the humming in Taos is that residents who hear it are actually registering noises created by their own ears. These spontaneous otoacoustic emissions are too low to hear over most everyday background noise, so people may not notice them until it's extremely quiet.

Another theory is that people who can detect the humming noise have an unusually strong sense of hearing. That would explain why only a small percentage of the overall population report hearing it. The sound could even be an auditory hallucination where people believe they hear something unusual because they've been preconditioned by rumors and reports.

[79]
THE HESSDALEN LIGHTS: NORWAY'S UNEXPLAINED LUMINOUS PHENOMENON

In the early 1980s, strange orbs of light started to manifest in the Hessdalen valley in Norway, sometimes appearing nearly two dozen times in a single day. The floating balls of light have persisted into the present day. At first, many people believed the lights were signs of extraterrestrial or paranormal activity, but they may yet have a scientific explanation.

Some lights grow as large as a car and remain for over an hour, while others seem to fly into the valley and vanish. The color can vary from white to blue, and they have almost a metal sheen in the daylight. Onlookers have recorded the orbs to document the bizarre phenomenon.

Project Hessdalen was formed in 1983 to study the behavior of the lights and their underlying cause. The group belongs to the Scientific Coalition for UAP Studies, and its research director is an astrophysicist with an interest in plasma physics and light emissions. Project Hessdalen also offers workshops that include instruction about how to use specialized equipment.

One theory is that minerals in the ground underneath the Hessdalen valley serve as a type of battery. The sulfur content in the river may cause a reaction and create the lights. The orbs could actually be ionized gas bubbles.

A researcher at Italy's Institute of Radio Astronomy tested this hypothesis by creating a model valley using rock samples taken from within the valley. When the model was exposed to sediment from the river, electricity flowed through it. More research is needed to fully understand how this results in the phenomena observed within the valley.

[80]
SKYQUAKES:
POSSIBLE EXPLANATIONS

A skyquake is an unexplained noise that resembles booming or extremely loud thunder. Skyquakes have been reported all over the world in locations ranging from Australia to Ireland. Some places even have their own terms to describe the sound. In Belgium, skyquakes are called *mistpoeffers*, meaning "fog guns."

James Fenimore Cooper, author of *The Last of the Mohicans*, described a skyquake in his short story "The Lake Gun." There are multiple theories about why skyquakes occur, but none have been definitively proven to be correct.

It's notable that most of the places where skyquakes have occurred are close to large bodies of water. This indicates water may play a role in how skyquakes are produced. Skyquakes have been reported in the vicinity of both freshwater and saltwater sources.

Skyquakes could also be caused by coronal mass ejections, a type of storm involving solar radiation. These storms can produce shock waves and accelerate protons, potentially creating sonic booms. This could explain why some people mistake them for the sonic booms caused by aircraft.

Natural phenomena like earthquakes and volcanoes can also generate sounds that travel long distances. In 2001, the earthquake that hit Spokane, Washington, created booms that sounded like explosions or artillery. Because of this, researchers have theorized that shifts in the continental shelf are responsible for skyquakes.

David Hill, an expert at the US Geological Survey, believes skyquakes could result from large waves disturbing pockets of methane hydrate along the ocean floor. When the pockets ignite, it causes loud booms. Despite the wealth of recordings and videos documenting skyquakes, further research is needed to determine the exact cause.

[81]
THE BLUE PEOPLE OF KENTUCKY: GENETICS OR AN UNKNOWN CONDITION?

In 1975, a child named Benjamin Stacy was born with noticeably blue skin. Doctors conducted a variety of tests but didn't find an underlying cause until the child's grandmother mentioned a hereditary condition that affected the extended family. It turned out to be methemoglobinemia, a rare condition where some of the hemoglobin in the body doesn't transport oxygen throughout the body.

The disorder was more widespread in Troublesome Creek, Kentucky, because of inbreeding. Since the area was extremely remote and didn't have reliable road access, the residents often married cousins who also carried the recessive gene. A researcher from the University of Indiana wrote about their blue skin in 1982, bringing more attention to the condition.

The color change caused by methemoglobinemia ranged from a bluish tinge to dark blue. Some people with the condition noticed the severity of the color lightening over time. Benjamin Stacy, for instance, grew out of having blue skin as a child. He may have only inherited the gene from one parent.

Eventually, the people affected by the condition in Troublesome Creek south sought out a hematologist at the University of Kentucky. The doctor discovered that injecting them with methylene blue dye would prompt the body to turn the methemoglobin into ordinary hemoglobin.

Methylene greatly improved the symptoms of the condition by addressing the fundamental underlying cause. Other possible treatments include vitamin C infusions and oxygen therapy in a hyperbaric chamber.

[82]
SPONTANEOUS HUMAN COMBUSTION: SCIENTIFIC THEORIES AND NOTABLE CASES

Accounts of spontaneous human combustion date back to the seventeenth century. The phenomenon was popularized in part by the Charles Dickens novel *Bleak House*. Since many victims in historical accounts were alcoholics or drinking, some reports speculated that alcohol saturation of the body played a role in cases of spontaneous human combustion.

According to modern science, that particular theory is impossible. Other purported causes include stress, electricity, and bacterial infections. One of the most recent examples is from 2010, when a coroner in Ireland determined that a 76-year-old man died of internal combustion. The man had been found dead from severe burns with no damage elsewhere in the room.

Scientists dispute that the original source of ignition in these cases is spontaneous combustion. Instead, they believe victims catch on fire through other means, and their clothing acts as a type of wick by soaking up melted fat. This could contain a fire and allow the body to smolder without fire spreading throughout the surrounding environment.

In 1998, researchers wrapped a dead pig in a blanket and lit it on fire to test the impact of fabric on a burning body. The resulting effect resembled how victims looked after reported instances of spontaneous combustion in humans.

If that hypothesis is correct, then alcohol could make the right conditions for fatal burns by reducing victims' ability to react quickly to an incipient fire. People who are extremely inebriated may also pass out and fall near a heat source. It's notable that the man who allegedly died of spontaneous combustion in Ireland was found near a fireplace.

Currently, there's no proof that the human body is capable of generating enough heat to cause spontaneous combustion. However, there simply aren't enough cases in modern times to study and draw concrete conclusions.

[83]
ANIMAL RAIN:
FROM FISH TO SPIDERS

As strange as it sounds, most cases of animal rain have natural causes. Extreme weather patterns or environmental conditions can affect animals in large numbers and alter their behavior in unusual ways. In some instances, it even causes them to fall from the sky like rain.

In Rákóczifalva, Hungary, frogs fell from the sky on two separate occasions in June 2010. After studying the incident, scientists concluded that a nearby tornado picked up the frogs and dropped them over Rákóczifalva.

Even routine weather changes have been known to cause animal rain. In Florida, some areas warn residents to watch out for falling iguanas when temperatures approach freezing. Since iguanas are intolerant of the cold, they freeze during cold weather and can't maintain their grips on trees and other surfaces.

However, not all cases of animal rain are so clear-cut. In the summer of 2007, earthworms fell from the sky in Jennings, Louisiana. Many of the worms were still alive. Witnesses wondered if it was the work of extraterrestrials or a sign of the apocalypse.

There have also been situations where a group of animals fell from the sky due to human interference in natural habitats. On New Year's Day in 2011, thousands of different birds dropped to the ground while flying over Arkansas. The birds belonged to several species, and they showed no outward signs of disease.

Investigators believe loud noises or an extreme change in the weather caused the birds to become disoriented. With global warming and weather patterns shifting, it's possible that more of these unusual events will occur in the future.

[84]
MARFA LIGHTS: ATMOSPHERIC REFLECTIONS OR THE UNEXPLAINED?

In Marfa, Texas, residents have noticed strange lights emanating from a remote area southeast of the town limits. The lights were first documented in 1883 when a ranch worker saw lights in the distance during a cattle drive. When locals went to investigate what they assumed were fires from Indigenous tribes, they didn't find any signs of a recent camp.

The lights continued to be seen throughout the twentieth century and into the present day. They sometimes appear in different colors, such as blue, red, and white. The lights aren't restricted to a particular time of year or temperature range, but they're more commonly seen at night when they have increased visibility.

Skeptics believe the lights are just visual distortions from headlights and campfires. Others claim they're made by the ghosts of Spanish conquistadors whose spirits roam the open desert outside Marfa.

There's also the possibility that gases like methane and phosphine are igniting after coming into contact with oxygen in the air. Similar phenomena have been observed in swampy regions. Although Marfa is located in a drastically different environment, petroleum in the area could produce a comparable effect under the right conditions.

An aerospace engineer who visited Marfa has also hypothesized that igneous rock generates an electric charge that causes the lights. A professor at Texas State University hasn't ruled out the hypothesis, stating there's simply not enough factual data to confirm an underlying cause at this time.

CHAPTER TEN: MYSTICAL PLACES

[85]
THE DEVIL'S SEA (DRAGON'S TRIANGLE): DISAPPEARANCES AND LEGENDS

The Devil's Sea encompasses the area around the island of Miyake, with three points touching Japan, the Philippines, and the Bonin Islands. Stories of the Devil's Sea extend as far back as 1274 CE, when it's rumored Kublai Khan lost his fleet and thousands of warriors to powerful storms during an attempted invasion of Japan.

Centuries later, multiple fishing vessels and military craft vanished in the Devil's Sea somewhere between the islands of Miyake and Iwo Jima. In 1952, the Japanese government sent a research vessel to investigate the cause. The ship was later found abandoned, but its 31 crew members were missing.

After that, Japan considered the Devil's Sea to be extremely dangerous for all types of vessels. So many ships have gone missing in the region that it's also known as the Pacific Bermuda Triangle. Some researchers consider the area to be one of a dozen "vile vortices," the places on the Earth where the electromagnetic forces are particularly strong. These forces could be caused by the intersection of currents with different temperatures.

Another theory suggests that the shipwrecks and other disappearances might be caused by underwater volcanic eruptions. It could also explain why sailors in the ancient world reported dragons living in the area that would suck ships into the sea. Deposits of methane hydrates support this hypothesis.

Others who have studied the Devil's Sea are convinced there are paranormal forces at work. Hundreds of people have lost their lives in mysterious cases throughout history, but it's unclear whether the cause is natural or some unknown phenomenon from beyond this world.

[86]
THE ZONE OF SILENCE: ANOMALIES AND STRANGE OCCURRENCES

The Zone of Silence is located in Mexico in a remote area of the Chihuahuan Desert. It's surrounded by the Mapimí Biosphere Reserve, a protected region with several endemic species like the bolson tortoise. Radio signals fail within the zone, which is roughly 31 miles across. Compasses also spin erratically when held close to stones.

Scientists believe the interference is caused by magnetite or debris left behind by meteorites. Three large meteorites fell within the zone between 1938 and 1969. Many people also believe the area has been visited by extraterrestrials and UFOs.

The area didn't earn its current name until 1966, when an oil company sent a team to explore the region. The leader of the group couldn't get his radio to work, causing him to start calling it the Zone of Silence.

This region of the Chihuahuan Desert gained even more notoriety in 1970 when a missile from a US Air Force base in Utah went hundreds of miles off course and impacted in the Zone of Silence. It was originally supposed to land at White Sands Missile Range in New Mexico. The US military promptly dispatched a team to recover the missile.

There are also rumors of extraterrestrials making themselves known. A UFO investigator in Chihuahua claims that people who get lost in the zone sometimes encounter tall beings with light-colored hair. The aliens allegedly speak fluent Spanish and ask humans for water before vanishing. They claim to be from somewhere "above."

[87]
THE BENNINGTON TRIANGLE: ANALYZING MAJOR DISAPPEARANCES

The Bennington Triangle, located around Vermont's Glastenbury Mountain, has repeatedly been the site of paranormal activity. From strange lights to UFOs, there's no shortage of examples from throughout the twentieth century. The greatest of its mysteries dates to the 1940s and 1950s when five people vanished within the triangle.

In the early nineteenth century, a group of stagecoach passengers were attacked by a large, hairy creature that resembled the description of Bigfoot. In 1943, a man named Carol Herrick was killed on a hunting trip by an unknown animal that left behind enormous footprints. Herrick's cause of death was squeezing.

Two years later, 74-year-old Middie Rivers disappeared after being separated from a group of hunters he was guiding through the area. Rivers had pushed on ahead of the others, but they never reconnected in the woods. Despite being an accomplished woodsman with years of experience, he was never seen again.

On October 28, 1950, a 53-year-old woman by the name of Freda Langer vanished while on a camping trip. Search parties combed the area for weeks but found nothing. Her body was discovered the following May in a place that had already been searched. Investigators weren't able to determine a cause of death.

Many others were lost in the woods in subsequent years. Some people believe it was the work of a prolific serial killer, while others believe the Bennington Triangle is a hotspot for the supernatural. According to stories from the Indigenous tribes in the region, the mountain itself is cursed. In Algonquin lore, an evil stone will open a hole and swallow up anyone who touches it.

[88]
SKINWALKER RANCH:
UFOS TO CRYPTIDS

Located in northeast Utah in the town of Gusher, Skinwalker Ranch is the site of countless paranormal occurrences. The ranch is considered to be such a hotspot of supernatural activity that it was even featured in a History Channel documentary.

According to legend, skinwalkers are witches who have shapeshifting powers. They can turn into any animal—or human. When Indigenous peoples occupied the land in Utah, the Navajo unleashed skinwalkers on the Ute tribe. It's said those skinwalkers still roam the area.

In 1994, Terry Sherman and his family bought the property that would later become Skinwalker Ranch. Sherman heard a suspicious noise outside one evening and went outside to investigate. He saw an enormous wolf and shot it several times. The animal appeared unfazed and soon ran off. Sherman chased after the creature, but its footprints suddenly vanished with no sign of the animal in sight.

Over their short two-year period of owning the ranch, the Shermans saw strange lights and objects throughout the property. They even found some of their cattle dead and mutilated. They sold the ranch to Robert Bigelow, a millionaire with an interest in the unexplained. Bigelow had just created the National Institute for Discovery Science, or NIDSci, an entity responsible for investigating UFOs and the paranormal.

Bigelow experienced many of the same phenomena reported by the Shermans. He eventually sold the ranch in 2016 to Brandon Fugal, a real estate investor who worked with the History Channel to document the oddities of Skinwalker Ranch.

Critics claim the UFOs and strange sightings are all fabricated, but some believers are convinced Skinwalker Ranch is a hub for otherworldly forces. A neuroscientist who studied the case also theorized that geophysical forces in the Uinta Basin can cause people to hallucinate.

[89]
THE NEVADA TRIANGLE: THE BERMUDA TRIANGLE'S COUNTERPART

Thousands of planes have gone missing over the Sierra Nevada Mountain range in an area known as the Nevada Triangle. The points of the triangle are located at Fresno, California; Las Vegas, Nevada; and Reno, Nevada. Area 51 is nearby, adding to the intrigue of this mysterious part of the country.

One theory of why planes go missing relates to Einstein's theory of space and time. Research by NASA indicates there could be rifts in spacetime itself due to the spinning of the Earth. This has caused some people to speculate that locations of unusual phenomena like the Nevada Triangle are actually portals that have opened in spacetime.

Skeptics point out that flying in the mountains is extremely challenging, and the weather conditions around the Sierra Nevada range can be unpredictable. It's possible that there's a higher number of crashes simply because of dangers in the surrounding environment. A pilot error could easily lead planes off course, especially in sudden storms or other high-risk settings.

However, even one of the world's most experienced pilots disappeared on a routine flight in the Nevada Triangle. Steve Fossett, the first person to fly around the world in a balloon, vanished on September 3, 2007. Rescuers searched for weeks without finding any evidence of Fossett's plane.

Just over a year later, a hiker found personal effects belonging to Fossett and notified the authorities. Search teams later found the crash site and Fossett's remains. Regardless of whether there are supernatural forces at work in the Nevada Triangle, it's clear that it's deadly territory no matter the cause.

[90]
HOIA-BACIU:
THE HAUNTED ROMANIAN FOREST

Although many tourists associate Transylvania with Bran Castle and Dracula, this region of Romania also houses the haunted forest of Hoia-Baciu. An area known as The Clearing is the most peculiar since nothing has grown there for years.

The forest's reputation dates back to 1968 when a man named Emil Barnea took a picture of a UFO hovering in the spot that would become The Clearing. Unlike other people who have claimed to see evidence of extraterrestrial life, Barnea brought his story to light at great personal risk. As a member of the military, he was connected to the Communist government, an entity that staunchly opposed any belief in the paranormal. Barnea subsequently lost his job after telling others about his photograph of the UFO.

Visitors to Hoia-Baciu have seen ghosts and experienced unusual sensations. Electronics sometimes fail to work properly, and tourists have reported feeling physically ill. There's even a local legend that a young girl vanished into the forest and reappeared years later, looking exactly the same as when she went missing.

Even the trees seem to show signs of unseen forces. Many grow in strange directions or spirals. Researchers haven't determined an exact cause for why this might happen. The trees that do spiral all turn clockwise.

According to tour guides who work regularly in the forest, some locals believe the power of Hoia-Baciu isn't necessarily evil. In their eyes, the forest is a reflection of the people who enter it, so having positive thoughts and making wishes for the future can harness the energies of Hoia-Baciu in a different way.

[91]
BRIDGEWATER TRIANGLE: A HUB OF PARANORMAL ACTIVITY

A 200-square-mile region of Massachusetts is renowned for being a hotspot of paranormal forces. The area is roughly triangular in shape, with points in Freetown, Rehoboth, and Abington. It encompasses the towns of Easton, Raynham, and Bridgewater, among others. It was dubbed the Bridgewater Triangle in 1983 by a cryptozoologist.

Some believe the strange phenomena in the triangle are caused by spirits left behind after King Philip's War, a bloody conflict between Indigenous peoples and British colonists that took place from 1675 to 1676. Up to three-quarters of the Indigenous combatants were killed, and the colonists lost a quarter of their forces.

Paranormal investigators note that people have seen glowing balls of light, cryptids like Bigfoot, and ghosts within the borders of the Bridgewater Triangle. Ordinary residents without an active interest in the supernatural have also reported unusual sightings and encounters.

In approximately 1990, a local man named Bill Russo was walking his dog in Raynham when he noticed what he originally thought was a child in a costume. The creature called to him and gestured for him to come closer. Russo quickly left because his dog was frightened, and he later discovered the creature he saw matched the description of a Pukwudgie, a mythical beast that lures its victims into the trees.

Some spirits even honor requests to prove their existence. The host of the podcast *Spooky Southcoast* dared the ghosts in the Lizzie Borden House to shove him against the wall and push him down the stairs. They were happy to oblige.

[92]
MOUNT RORAIMA:
LEGENDS OF A LOST WORLD

Mount Roraima is located at the intersection of Brazil, Venezuela, and Brazil. It's both the highest point in Guyana and the tallest plateau of the flat-topped Pakaraima Mountains. In Sir Arthur Conan Doyle's 1912 novel *The Lost World*, the characters climb Mount Roraima and discover that supposedly extinct creatures have survived on the plateaus.

The story isn't exactly fiction. Rare flora and fauna have actually been found on Mount Roraima. Up to 35 percent of the animals found on the mountain are endemic, meaning they're only found in an extremely limited area.

The species at the top are particularly rare and at risk, since it's so difficult to traverse between the top and bottom of the mountain. The Roraima black frog, for example, can only be found on Mount Roraima. It's probable that multiple new species have yet to be discovered.

The Pemón people who originally lived in the region believed Mount Roraima used to be a great tree that created all fruits and vegetables. When a Pemón ancestor cut down the tree, it flooded the region and created the rivers that flow throughout the area. Mount Roraima is said to be the stump of that great tree.

With sheer walls nearly a quarter mile in height, Mount Roraima is inhospitable and difficult to access. The first person to ascend the plateau was Sir Everard im Thurn in 1884. The Pemón people used to warn that anyone who attempted to climb Mount Roraima would perish.

Modern-day visitors to the plateau have reported experiencing unusual sensations. Some people claim the energy on Mount Roraima is similar to the kind found in other supernatural places such as the Bermuda Triangle.

[93]
AOKIGAHARA FOREST: THE DARK ALLURE OF JAPAN'S HAUNTED FOREST

The Aokigahara forest is also known as the Sea of Trees or, more insidiously, the "suicide forest." Located just over 80 miles west of Tokyo, the forest runs alongside Mount Fuji. Since few animals live within the forest, it's incredibly quiet within the densely crowded trees. The forest's history of suicide and its silence both add to its reputation as a haunted forest.

Because of the high number of suicides in the Aokigahara forest, the Japanese government has stopped releasing exact statistics to avoid drawing further attention to the area. The most recent figures from between 2013 and 2015 indicate that over 100 people from outside the region traveled to the Aokigahara forest to commit suicide.

The government has also implemented safety measures such as installing cameras to monitor entry points to the forest. There are even signs posted to remind visitors that help is available for anyone who's feeling suicidal. Yet, as a country, Japan continues to have relatively high rates of suicide compared to other developed nations. In 2022, there were 17.5 suicides for every 100,000 people in Japan.

Researchers and mental health professionals have spent years trying to determine why people flock to the forest to take their own lives. Some people who have attempted suicide but survived state they sought out a place to die where they wouldn't be interrupted or discovered. Others mentioned they didn't want to feel alone, and they thought a forest famous for suicides would allow them to be accepted in death.

CHAPTER ELEVEN:
ENIGMATIC INDIVIDUALS

[94]
D.B. COOPER:
THE INFAMOUS SKYJACKER WHO VANISHED

On November 24, 1971, a man named D.B. Cooper boarded a flight from Portland, Oregon, to Seattle, Washington, with a one-way ticket. Once they were in the air, Cooper passed the flight attendant a note explaining he had a bomb. He showed the flight attendant his carry-on bag, which contained wires and other components resembling explosives. His demands were simple: $200,000 in cash and four parachutes.

The flight crew alerted the FBI to the situation, and the FBI, in turn, reached out to the airline. The president of the company asked the FBI to give Cooper what he wanted. Cooper had clearly researched the entire hijacking in great detail. He requested $20 bills with random serial numbers and would only accept civilian models of parachutes.

When the plane landed, he traded the passengers for the ransom, but he made the three people in the cockpit and a flight attendant stay behind. Cooper was also extremely knowledgeable about flight and the aircraft in general. He instructed the pilot to head to Mexico City. He also helped chart the course and set the plane's speed and altitude.

Cooper told all personnel to remain in the cockpit. They had no way of observing the rest of the plane, so they couldn't be positive about when Cooper jumped. Although the door opened just before 8:30 p.m., he could have been bluffing and exited the plane at a later point. When the alert sounded about the open door, the plane was only a short distance from Portland.

In 1980, a young boy found a bundle of cash that matched the ransom money given to Cooper. This caused investigators to theorize that he didn't survive the jump. Many people have claimed to have knowledge of D.B. Cooper's identity, but none of those cases have been substantiated.

[95]
THE BABUSHKA LADY AT THE JFK ASSASSINATION: WHO WAS SHE?

The assassination of President John F. Kennedy is one of the defining moments of American history. An astounding number of people believe it was a conspiracy, and interest in JFK's death has remained into the present day. The videos and photographs from the crowd have become famous and provided much of the direct evidence of how the shooting occurred.

However, there's one witness who has never been identified. A woman with a camera appears in several now-famous recordings by people like Mark Bell and Orville Nix, but no one matching her description came forward with footage in the aftermath of the assassination. The woman was wearing a headscarf reminiscent of Russian grandmothers, so observers nicknamed her the "Babushka Lady."

She was watching the presidential procession from a grassy area between Elm and Main Street. That placed her in front of the Dallas County Building for at least part of the motorcade. Even though most people dispersed after shots were fired, the Babushka Lady kept taking pictures or recording.

Given the angle of her arms and the fact that she didn't move when others crouched down or ran, researchers are fairly confident she was holding a video camera rather than taking still photographs.

After she was done, she continued down Elm Street with the crowd and vanished.

Some historians believe the Babushka Lady might actually be two different people. She appears in front of the Dallas County Building and then later in Dealey Plaza. In order to appear in both locations, she would have needed to cross the street. As more time goes on, it becomes less likely that the Babushka Lady will ever be identified.

[96]
THE IDENTITY OF JACK THE RIPPER: A CENTURY-LONG MANHUNT

Jack the Ripper is one of the most famous serial killers in history. From August to November 1888, he killed at least five women in the East London district of Whitechapel. Additional murders that occurred in the area are difficult to definitively link to Jack the Ripper because of discrepancies in how the attacks were carried out.

The physical descriptions of Jack the Ripper vary widely. A woman who saw Jack the Ripper's second victim just before her death noted that she was accompanied by a man with dark hair, a deerstalker hunting hat, and a dark-colored coat. Another witness who passed through the site of Catherine Eddowes's murder just before she was attacked stated she was in the presence of a man with fair hair and an average build.

In 2014, a book by Russell Edwards pointed the finger at Aaron Kosminski, a 23-year-old barber who was also investigated by the police in the aftermath of the murders. Edwards claims that semen found on Catherine Eddowes's shawl matches DNA samples from Kosminski's modern-day relatives.

Experts criticized Edwards's analysis after he refused to release the full details of the DNA testing. They also questioned the use of mitochondrial DNA, stating that mitochondrial DNA is only reliable to rule out the possibility of a familial connection. It can't be used to establish a genetic link.

A police volunteer believes a man named Hyam Hyams might be responsible for the murders. She used records about Hyams's work, health, and home life to establish a link. Hyams also had injuries that prevented him from walking properly, which matched witness descriptions claiming Jack the Ripper had a stilted gait. Notably, the murders in Whitechapel stopped shortly after Hyams was taken into police custody and transferred to a mental institution.

[97]
THE ISDAL WOMAN: MULTIPLE FALSE IDENTITIES AND HER UNSOLVED DEATH

On November 29, 1970, a man and his two young daughters were hiking in Isdalen Valley, an area just outside of Bergen, Norway, when they discovered the body of a dead woman. She was badly burned and lying on her back. When the police came to investigate, they had no idea they were inadvertently becoming involved in one of the strangest deaths of the century.

Law enforcement found the woman's belongings nearby. Many of them were burned, and all the labels had been removed. They found an umbrella, a passport cover, pieces of clothing, and several bottles. The woman's watch and jewelry had also been placed off to the side.

The case grew even more complicated when police found a fingerprint belonging to the Isdal woman on a pair of glasses in a suitcase left behind at the train station. None of her clothes or cosmetics had labels, and there was an encoded note in her bag.

Police discovered she'd been using multiple aliases while staying in different hotels. The woman had also been carrying currencies from several different countries, indicating she might have been traveling throughout Europe for some time or planning to return to other locations. This led law enforcement personnel to consider whether she was a spy.

However, the official ruling is that her death was a suicide since her stomach was found to contain dozens of sleeping pills. She was burned alive using gasoline before many of them had entered her bloodstream.

One of the original investigators later claimed few people supported the official conclusion. Some officers kept researching the case. In fact, the evidence for suicide was so flimsy that the Norwegian police agreed to reopen the case in 2016 to see if modern forensics might yield new clues about the Isdal Woman's death.

[98]
KASPAR HAUSER:
THE BOY WHO APPEARED FROM NOWHERE

In May of 1828, a boy named Kaspar Hauser appeared in modern-day Nuremberg, Germany, carrying two letters and no other possessions. The letters were from his mother and an unknown caregiver who had once taken him in. They said he had no one who could look after him anymore, and they hoped Hauser would be able to join the military.

Hauser didn't know how to read or write anything except his name. He seemed accustomed to meals of water and bread rather than eating anything else offered to him. He also lacked any familiarity with basic manners or the conventions of living in a civilized society.

Therefore, people were astounded when the boy learned to read and write in a matter of weeks. His story gained so much attention that he wrote and published an autobiography explaining his upbringing. Hauser claimed that he'd been kept in a dark room and hadn't been able to interact with any of the people who'd taken care of him.

Hauser's notoriety only grew when multiple people attempted to kill him with seemingly no cause. In 1833, he was stabbed to death by an unknown assailant. These unusual details caused some to speculate that Hauser was really the heir to a throne, and he'd been locked away to prevent him from claiming his rightful place.

Other theories were that Hauser suffered from mental illness after being abused during his childhood. Some people even claimed he had epilepsy, which caused his unusual habits. However, those theories didn't explain why assassins would be interested in taking the life of an otherwise unremarkable teenage boy.

[99]
THE COUNT OF ST. GERMAIN: THE MAN WHO CLAIMED TO BE CENTURIES OLD

The Count of St. Germain was born in the late 1600s or early 1700s. The story goes that Countess von Georgy heard about the Count of St. Germain visiting Paris in 1760. When she met him, she pointed out that she'd encountered a man with the same title in Italy in 1710. The countess assumed she'd met his father, but the Count of St. Germain insisted he knew her and that he was unnaturally old despite his much younger appearance.

Since the count was an accomplished alchemist, his contemporaries in the eighteenth century wondered if he'd discovered the philosopher's stone and gained immortality. The Count of St. Germain also seemed to have more knowledge than one person could acquire in a lifetime. He spoke several languages fluently, including German, Arabic, Russian, and Chinese.

It's also intriguing that royals and famous figures from throughout Europe were familiar with the Count of St. Germain. He traveled extensively, and rumors claim he assisted rulers such as Louis XV of France and Catherine the Great. Voltaire even wrote about the count, albeit his description may have been somewhat sarcastic.

In 1779, the Count of St. Germain traveled to Germany and stayed for five years with Prince Charles of Hesse-Cassel. He died in the castle at Eckernförde in late February 1784. However, despite the historical record of his death, the count continued to appear throughout Europe.

Records indicate that the Freemasons selected the count to serve as their representative to a gathering in 1785. In 1821, the writer Albert Vandam claimed the count had changed his name to Major Fraser. At the end of the nineteenth century, the mystic Helena Blavatsky supposedly took a picture with the Count of St. Germain, but no copies have ever been found.

[100]
THE LADY OF DAI:

THE WELL-PRESERVED MUMMY WITH AN ENIGMATIC PAST

The Lady of Dai, also known as Xin Zhui, was buried near present-day Changsha, China. Construction workers discovered her tomb — and those of her husband and another close relative — while digging into a hill in 1971 to create an emergency air-raid shelter. The Lady of Dai would become one of the most famous mummies ever found because of how remarkably well-preserved her body is compared to others of the same age.

The Lady of Dai lived from 206 BCE to 220 CE during the Han dynasty, making her mummy roughly 2,100 years old at the time of discovery. She was married to Li Cang, a nobleman who held the title Marquis of Dai.

The Lady of Dai's mummy is in such incredible condition that her skin is still soft, and her limbs move. Her eyelashes, hair, and organs are intact as well. There's even still blood in her circulatory system.

Archaeologists have several theories about the Lady of Dai's condition. It's possible her body was protected enough from the environment and oxygen to avoid decomposition. She was found inside of four nested coffins that were each covered in lacquer and a silk painting. Inside, the Lady of Dai was buried in 18 layers of clothing made of silk and cotton.

A clear liquid found inside the coffin may also have played a role. The liquid turned brown after the coffin was opened, indicating it had kept out the air prior to being excavated. Some researchers think the liquid might be bodily secretions from after death, but others claim it's a type of solution made with Chinese herbs to preserve the body.

[101]
LORI ERICA RUFF:
THE WOMAN WITH TWO IDENTITIES

Tragedy struck on December 24, 2010, when Lori Erica Ruff took her own life outside her home in Longview, Texas. Her husband, Blake, had recently filed for divorce and was temporarily living with his parents. Ruff had been threatening her husband and acting strangely before committing suicide on Christmas Eve.

When Blake started going through his wife's possessions, he found a lockbox in the closet that Ruff had warned him not to touch. When he opened it, he discovered a birth certificate and multiple IDs with different names. It turned out Lori Erica Ruff had been living under false names and identities throughout her life.

Before Ruff got married, she went under the alias Lori Erica Kennedy. Prior to that, she used the name Becky Sue Turner after acquiring the birth certificate of a toddler who died in a Seattle house fire in 1971. Once she'd successfully obtained a driver's license as Becky Sue Turner, she legally changed her name and moved to Dallas.

Blake's family had always had their doubts about Ruff. She'd been unusually secretive about her past and claimed that her parents had already passed away. The situation worsened after Ruff gave birth to a daughter in 2008 and attempted to limit how often Blake's family could see her.

The truth about Ruff's real identity wouldn't be uncovered until 2016 when an investigator for Social Security received a tip that Ruff had a DNA match with a first cousin who lived in Philadelphia. The investigator traveled to Pennsylvania and showed the family a picture of Ruff. They immediately identified her as Kimberly McLean, a long-missing Pennsylvania woman who'd last been seen at the age of 18 when she'd threatened to run away.

CONCLUSION

As you now see, history is full of strange occurrences that span thousands of years and countless cultures. Our knowledge of the greater universe remains limited at best, so it's only natural to stumble upon a mystery every now and then. As time goes on, new conundrums will join the likes of Jack the Ripper, Mount Roraima, and the Borley Rectory.

The Greatest Mysteries in History is only the first step on your journey to uncover the truth about bizarre coincidences and unusual creatures. Whether you take a crack at an unsolved cipher or study a particular mystery for yourself, don't lose the sense of curiosity that first led you to pick up this book.

There's a wealth of new information every year about many of these enigmatic historical events, so keep an open mind as you continue to research unexplained phenomena. A single missing link could be all that's needed to unlock the truth. In some cases, scientific limitations are part of the reason these unbelievable encounters and baffling discoveries have continued to confound the leading experts of their time.

It may take more research and advanced technologies to fully understand many of the mysteries you read about in these chapters. Some may even change our ideas about the nature of human history, the existence of the paranormal, and whether we really are alone in the universe.

Made in the USA
Middletown, DE
07 December 2024

66299033R00080